the Tabernacle of Moses

The Prototype for Salvation in Jesus Christ

DR. HENRY HORTON

WESTBOW®
PRESS
A DIVISION OF THOMAS NELSON
& ZONDERVAN

WestBow Press books may be ordered through booksellers or by contacting:

WestBow Press
A Division of Thomas Nelson & Zondervan
1663 Liberty Drive
Bloomington, IN 47403
www.westbowpress.com
1 (866) 928-1240

Editorial services provided by *The Good Word*, April Mosby, Copy Editor

All scriptural quotations, unless otherwise noted, are
from the King James version of the Bible.

ISBN: 978-1-4908-2282-2 (sc)
ISBN: 978-1-4908-2283-9 (hc)
ISBN: 978-1-4908-2281-5 (e)

Library of Congress Control Number: 2014903036

Printed in the United States of America.

WestBow Press rev. date: 4/4/2014

Dedication Page

This book is dedicated:

To my wife:
Dr. Karen Horton, the most wonderful woman God ever created.

To our children:
Paulette Francis; Jerome Horton and wife Yvonne;
Glenda Sherman; Major Horton; Gloria Harold and
husband Glenn; Vincent Greer and wife, Pring;

To our grandchildren:
Myeshia Horton; Matthew Horton; Myles Harold; Maya
Harold; Sydney Horton; Kia Horton; and Tina Johnson.

To our great-grandchildren:
Carolyn Johnson and Sahara Horton

To our sisters:
Verna M. Holt and Earnestine Horton.

To our nieces and nephews:
Dr. Henry Horton, MD; Karen Horton; Kevin Horton;
Lorena Abarca; Dontis Williams; Marvin Williams Jr.;
Michael Williams; Marlon Williams; Monica Williams,
and husband Daniel Williams and daughter Zoe.

**To our Senior Pastor at Maranatha
Community Church and his wife:**

Senior Pastor Steven W. Dyson and Wife, Reatha Dyson

And most importantly to:

Almighty God In three persons: the Father, Son, and Holy Spirit.

Affectionate Mentions:

To the loving memory of:

*Mr. Milas Green, Chief Financial Officer CLLC Ministries;
Milas was a dearly beloved brother in Christ, who loved
God, his family and his church. Known simply as Milas,
he was a servant to mankind and he was my friend.*

To living Senior Mentors:

*Master Deacon Maranatha Community Church
Deacon Robert Thomas*

*Pastor New Brighter Day Church
Senior Pastor E.C. Bowdry*

Affectionate Inspirations

*I am privileged to draw great inspiration from the church
mothers of Maranatha Community Church:*

Mother Anna Ingram; Mother Mae Brown; Mother Rosetta
Wicker; Mother Barbbie Johnson; Mother Mary Ann Montaque;
Mother Celestine Wilburn; Mother Cecilia Nwobie; Mother
Carolyn Hamilton; Mother Otha L. Anderson; Mother Ernestine
Holmes; Mother Florence Johnson; Mother Sheryl Solomon.

Contents

To the Students of 2012-2013 Class: How to Effectively Study the Bible and the Tabernacle

Abrams, Mary; Abrams, Tommy; Anderson, Betty; Anderson, Queen, Victoria; Ballenger, Alonzo; Bellot, Noreen; Barner, Robert R., Ph.D.; Board, John; Brisco, Shelly; Board, Odette; Borders William; Bowman, Cheryl ; Brown, Ann, Minister; Brown, Robert; Brown, Tina; Burgess, Jimmie; Burgess, Tiffany; Burgess,Vicki; Burrus, Rogena Fulcher, Minister; Carter, Angela; Carter, Anika; Chin, Rebecca; Christian, Michelle; Cole Edwina; Dexter, Louvetta; Dickerson, Clifford; Dyson, Mrs. Reatha; Ellis, Lisa, Minister; Ellis, Russell, Minister; Ellis, Troya; Evans, Gloria; Fair, Joslyn; Fair, Timothy; Franklin, Dovema, Pastor; Franklin, Ken; Franklin, Toni, Minister; Frazier, Gina; Freelow, Darren; Hawkins, Joy; Hawkins, Hopkins, Terri; Henry, Stacy; Hines, Angela; Horn, Larry; Horn, Vanessa; Ingram, Carolyn; Jackson, Jai Renee; Johnson, Barbbie, Mother ; Johnson, Renee; Johnson, Wendell; Irving, Agnes; Jones, Judy; Jordan, Carl; Langley, Norman; Lester, Tina; Lestric, Donnie; Marshall, Gloria; Marshall, Jordan; Martin, Gloria; Martin, Lindzie; Miles, Michael; Montaque, Mary Ann, Mother ; McCall, Linda; McKinney, Lisley; Montaque, Dawn; Montaque, Joy; Moore, Anthony; Morgan, Attila; Morgan, Charles, Pastor; Mosby, April, Minister; Nebedum, Waverly; Nelms, Frank; Niigwe, Patricia; Norris, Carol; Ogamba, Donah Kelly; Ogwonuwe, Kimberly; Andrian, Oliver; Parker, Renee; Philips, Shannon; Phillinganes, Karal; Price Ron; Richardson, Egzine; Riera, Sylvia; Rutherford , Reggie; Scott, Benny,

Usher ; Shamsiddeen, Ikie; Simpson, Elaine; Smith, Kenneth; Solomon, Richard Minister; Somerville, Larcita; Spencer, Patricia; Stephens, Charles; Stephens, Patrice; Stevenson, Robert; Stevenson, Roz; Street, Bridgette; Taylor, Terri; Taylor, Wanda; Thomas, Cynthia, Pastor; Glenda Thomas; Tudor, Inger; Vinson, Deidra, Vinson; Waldron, Carmen; Ware, Dorothy; Warren, Michelle ; Wilburn, Celestine, Mother ; Wicker, Rosetta, Mother; Wilhite, Patricia; Williams, Patricia; Wright, Deborah.

Our Spiritual Sons and Daughters:

Burrus, Aaron, Los Angeles; Cochran, Kenneth and Retta, Pastors, Flint, MI; Cordett, Jerry, Los Angeles; Fisher, Earl Pastor, Flint, MI; Grays, Doloris Minister Flint, MI; Griggs, Lamar Supt., Flint, MI; Howard, Kenneth Ph.D., and Tawana Pastors, Detroit, MI; Larkin, LaRoi and Ashley, Ministers, Los Angeles; Strater, Andre Minister Flint, MI; Thomas, Cynthia Pastor Los Angles; Marshall Quinten Supt., Flint, MI; Wiggins, Donald and Cookie Minister Islamorada, Florida; Williams, Michael Golf Pro. Los Angeles.

Acknowledgments

My deepest thanks go to my wife, Dr. Karen Horton, for many hours of dedicated skill, biblical research and teaching assistance … Thanks to: Paulette Francis; Jerome and Yvonne Horton; Major Horton; Glanda Sherman; and Glen and Gloria Harold; for encouragement, editorial and structural feedback on the book... Thanks to Mr. Lamaud Franklin; Ricky Gadbury; Shirese Hursey; Vernessie Horn, and Forrest Asbury for copying and recording the work… My thanks to the Photography Consultants: Myeshia Horton and Queen Victoria Anderson.

Preface

Having invested more than thirty years studying this old structure at Mount Sinai called the Tabernacle of Moses, and being privileged by father God to teach the Tabernacle of Moses, I was prompted to search for a connection, a link, if you will, between the New Testament believer and this Old Testament Tabernacle in the Sinai wilderness. I wanted to learn what, if any, relationship, importance, and/or significance, this outdated, natural, and symbolic structure, with all its rituals and traditions of sacrificing bulls, goats, doves, heifers etc., had to the substitutionary sacrifice of Jesus Christ on Calvary's cross. The reward of that search was more than I ever thought it would be and, even now, God continues to pour out revelation regarding the many connections between these two monumental and historical events. That study led me to write: ***"The Tabernacle of Moses: the Prototype for Salvation in Jesus Christ"***. The book is intended to be a source for better understanding the Tabernacle in the wilderness and how God used it and its sacrificial rituals to create the pathway for the believer's salvation in Christ Jesus. The explanation and documentation of this scriptural, historical record will, without a doubt, open for many the understanding of all scripture in both the Old and New Testaments.

The Foreword

In our church, I witnessed firsthand the birthing of "The Tabernacle of Moses: the Prototype for Salvation in Jesus Christ" as Dr. Henry Horton, with careful and thoughtful tenacity for scriptural accuracy, taught and explained from the Word of God, the ceremonies, washings, blood sacrifices, duties, and functions of the various priests, non-priests, women, animals, furnishings, and utensils of this Old Testament Tabernacle. Further, I watched the enthusiastic diligence and growth of our membership as many of them, for the first time, began to see more clearly the mind of God at work in this Old Testament Tabernacle experience. It was highly instructional as Dr. Horton made it clear from the scriptures that God was establishing a way for sinful mankind, who walked away from God in the Garden of Eden, to come back to him through the shedding of the blood of a sacrificial substitute.

Now, as one who is privileged to extract from the many scriptural implications and lessons of the Tabernacle of Moses in the Sinai desert, and seeing the broader more receptive atmosphere in our congregation to a new level of teaching, I highly recommend the reading of "The Tabernacle of Moses: the Prototype for Salvation in Jesus Christ". I know firsthand that this book will enhance your understanding and appreciation of the scriptures in both the Old and New Testaments.

Dr. Horton's demand for scriptural accuracy, and his direct, but simple and practical explanation of the Word of God, should be experienced by every believer before they leave this earth. "The Tabernacle of Moses: the Prototype for Salvation in Jesus Christ", like nothing else I have read or heard, is sure to increase your understanding and appreciation for the sacrifice that Jesus made at the cross for salvation.

We are pleased that Dr. Horton and his lovely wife, Karen Horton, are active members of Maranatha Community Church.

Steven W. Dyson, Senior Pastor
Maranatha Community Church

Reader's Guide

"The Tabernacle of Moses: the Prototype for Salvation in Jesus Christ" is a theological, historical, and scriptural explanation of the Tabernacle of Moses in the Sinai wilderness. It is an in-depth and engaging work that examines every detail of this Old Testament Tabernacle; and we glean from every aspect of the Tabernacle story, a connection with Jesus Christ. As I studied this old structure, seeking to learn its connection to the redemptive work of Jesus Christ, it seemed I was being taken on a journey back into time. My desire was to take others by the hand and guide them along to where God revealed the most amazing, illuminating, and startling connections of the old Tabernacle blood-shed, to the work of our savior at Golgotha. What God has revealed here is intensely transformative. It unlocks long-hidden secrets, whose discovery prepares hearts for truth we have never known. It pours into our understanding the immensely revealing connections that leave no doubt as to why the Tabernacle of Moses was the prerequisite for the coming Messiah, our Savior Jesus Christ.

The average truth seeker, Christian or not, without a theological background will find this book a helpful guide for understanding the present day importance of this Old Testament structure. The Tabernacle of Moses was a portable sanctuary where God chose to come and dwell on earth among his people (*see Exodus 25:8*). The Israelites had been in bondage in Egypt for over four-hundred years, but God had freed them through the Red Sea experience, and they now journeyed from Egypt, toward a place identified to them only as the Promised Land. They lived in tents and so the Tabernacle was also a tent.

"*The Tabernacle of Moses: the Prototype for Salvation in Jesus Christ*" explains how God, in his wisdom, reveals the Tabernacle story to man using primarily the Bible books of Exodus, Leviticus, Numbers, Deuteronomy, and Hebrews. Ultimately he uses the entire Bible to teach through types, shadows, and symbols, the importance of this Tabernacle structure, its attendants, and ceremonies, in the development of the religious life of Israel, and its importance to our lives today.

There is great and significant purpose for mankind today in what God did in this Old Testament structure. The book you now hold in your hands, with careful and explicit clarity, helps us understand how the redeeming work of Jesus Christ, is a direct outgrowth of the Tabernacle experience.

Here are twelve (12) questions book clubs and reading groups might use:

(1)   When did mankind recognize they were naked?

(2)   Why did God create mankind and what scripture supports your answer?

(3)   What is it that mankind often chooses to obey as opposed to revelation from God?

(4)   Why did God cover Adam and Eve in the Garden of Eden with the skin of an animal?

(5)   Why is the statement, "Without the shedding of blood there is no remission for sin" true? Where in the book of Leviticus is there scripture to support this statement?

(6)   Who were the priests in the tribe of Levi?

(7)   Did God ever move? If not, why not? If he did, how would his followers know to follow him?

(8)   Who killed the sacrificial animal at the altar: the priest or the sinner?

(9)   The substitutionary sacrifices in the tabernacle were goats, bulls, heifers etc. Name the substitutionary sacrifice for present day mankind?

(10) Who constitutes the present-day priesthood that replaced the old tabernacle priesthood?

(11) What do you know about Jesus that you did not know before you read this book?

(12) What do you know about yourself that you did not know before you read this book?

INTRODUCTION

Much of the true meaning of *God's Word* which we read in the Bible is meaningless without some knowledge and understanding of the concealed messages of this Old Testament tabernacle. The entire Bible, including the principles of atonement, forgiveness, sacrifice and salvation, is built on the services and ceremonies demonstrated in this structure. Yet, the Tabernacle teaching is one of the most neglected areas of study for many believers. The body of Christ, the church, suffers from ignorance concerning the spiritual realities found in the hidden mysteries in the bloody, sacrificial approach to atonement that God established in the Tabernacle of Moses.

The revealing of this old tabernacle approach to redemption for sinful man starts with God's instructions to Moses: *"And let them make me a sanctuary; that I may dwell among them. According to all that I shewed thee, after the pattern of the tabernacle, and the pattern of all the instruments thereof, even so shall ye make it" (Exodus 25:8–9).*

This book is informed and guided by the scriptures based on the fact that God speaks to his people through his Word. We hear Timothy say: *"All scripture is given by inspiration of God, and is profitable for doctrine, for reproof, for correction, for instruction in righteousness, that the man of God may be perfect, thoroughly furnished unto all good* works" *(2 Timothy 3:16–17)*. And further, the scriptures admonish and instruct all mankind to*: "Study to show yourself approved unto God, a workman that needs not to be ashamed, rightly dividing the word of truth" (2 Timothy 2:15)*. As we approach this study, or the study of the Word at any time, we find in the Word a fitting prayer: *"Open thou mine eyes, that I may behold wondrous things out of thy law"* (Psalm 119:18).

Our mantra during the study will be the words of Proverbs 25:2: *"It is the glory of God to conceal a thing: but the honour of kings is to search out a matter."* To paraphrase, it is the prerogative of God to conceal things; however, as kings and priests, it is the believer's duty to search out these concealed mysteries. The scriptures clearly identify believers as kings and priests: *"And hath made us kings and priests unto God and his father; to him be glory and dominion for ever and ever Amen."* Also, *"And they sung a new song, saying, Thou art worthy to take the book, and to open the seals thereof: for thou wast slain, and hast redeemed us to God by thy blood out of every kindred, and tongue, and people, and nation; And hast made us unto our God kings and priests: and we shall reign on the earth"* *(Revelation 5:9–10)*. So, it is the believer's honor, rather his duty, to search out these mysteries; they are guides for our spiritual relationships with God and mankind.

We will study the Tabernacle as God revealed it to Moses. Through the tabernacle, God gave instructions to the nation of Israel and for mankind today. The study is an in-depth review of the tabernacle's structure, furnishings, materials, ceremonies, sacrifices and people, and we will review how every element is connected to Jesus Christ. We must always remember that God's Word is its own commentary, its own interpreter. Therefore, in our study of the tabernacle, we will follow his Word, allowing the scriptures to take their free course and guide us to truth and new revelation. Here, we will refer to the tabernacle as the *"Tabernacle of Moses"* to distinguish it from other tabernacles mentioned in scriptures, such as the tabernacles of David, Solomon's temples, etc. It must always be clear in our understanding that the original tabernacle pattern was given by God to Moses, and the entire nation of Israel functioned around this Tabernacle structure for nearly four-hundred years. Why is this tabernacle so important? How could gold, silver, brass, wood, and skins be so important in the lives of God's people? It is important because it was where God chose to dwell on earth, where he gave direction to the religious life of Israel, and where he demonstrated his accepted way for sinful humans to return to him. It was in this tabernacle that man witnessed the substitute-blood-sacrifices, the washings and cleansings in preparation for atonement. It was also in this tabernacle that God gave guidance and instructions for the nation of Israel to live by; these instructions offered types, shadows and patterns for the church today.

It is a well-established fact that the intelligent human thought process requires a foundation of knowledge to support the human belief system and to undergird the rationale needed to build the next phase of one's understands. You have embarked upon a truly wonderful scriptural journey into the mysteries of ancient times, lands, languages, histories, and chronologies of the infallible Word of God.

"The Tabernacle of Moses: the Prototype for Salvation in Jesus Christ" presents an unusual learning experience. I applaud your wisdom to discern and follow the leading of God's spirit as he directs your next level of spiritual growth and understanding.

Preparing the Mind for Truth

The path to great benefits from an examination of scripture, or any subject for that matter, is to start at the beginning of the proposed matter, and move sequentially through to the end. That may seem obvious, however, many of us have been taught the scriptures in choppy bits and pieces that never link with other supplementary and instructive scripture. Orderly linking of the gospel message together will improve our understanding immensely.

Clarity of the tabernacle teaching will require that we cover a number of major biblical events. Clarity also demands that we link these events in a logical sequence, presenting one continuous message, so that by the time the reader finishes this book, the scriptures and events we cover will make sense and your understanding of the entire Holy Bible will have grown by leaps. The purpose of this work is to help us clearly understand the Tabernacle of Moses and the truth that God has concealed there, to show its foundational importance for the coming of the Messiah, and to increase our understanding of all scripture.

For clear scriptural understanding to occur, we must understand and accept that God is a spirit; He is not to be beheld as a natural man (see John 4:21–24). Here, our Lord Jesus Christ converses with a woman at the well in the city of Samaria. She is called in scripture the

Samaritan woman. This is the same woman he spoke to about her five husbands. Jesus and the woman discussed the proper place to worship God: *"Jesus saith unto her woman, believe me, the hour cometh, when ye shall neither in this mountain, nor yet at Jerusalem, worship the father. Ye worship ye know not what: we know what we worship: for salvation is of the Jews, but the hour cometh and now is, when the true worshippers shall worship the father in spirit and in truth: for the father seeketh such to worship him. God is a spirit: and they that worship him must worship him in spirit and in truth."*

Here, Jesus is teaching several things. First, God is not impressed with our place of worship and secondly, godly worship, is led by our spiritual devoutness and attitude. When the Lord says, "we must worship him in spirit and in truth," he is saying, true worship can occur only at a level of spiritual commitment that most humans do not understand. Authentic worship originates in the spirit of humanity and is an expression of a deep inner devotion and obedience to God.

The most important statement of the master in this passage is this: ***"For the father seeketh such to worship him"*** Listen, the almighty, self-sufficient God of all creation does not seek the attention of humanity at any other place in scripture. The God who says, "If I were hungry, I wouldn't tell you," here, is seeking humankind, you and me, to worship him. Awesome!

A person who truly experiences the revelation of God's Word, is immediately drawn to a deeper appreciation of the Master. They realize that God alone is the combination of commitment, power and love essential to save and deliver them from their uncertain fears, confusion, and frustrations. True comprehension of the word of scripture inspires a new appreciation of God that stimulates humans to a level of admiration and acceptance of God for who he is, for what he does, and for his unconditional love for mankind.

Only by the leading of the spirit of God, without human intervention, will the persuaded, admiring, and submitted believer become a worshipper. Supernatural, spiritual understanding based on revelation produces the faith for acceptance of truth. When we are yielded to God, He causes our human spirit to bear witness with the Holy Spirit. When that happens, humans cannot resist the call of God to worship him, as his spirit leads, teaches, and guides us into all truth regarding salvation, godliness, and life on earth. It is amazing how sweet life becomes when we seek his true revelation and walk after the spirit of our maker.

Unfortunately, misguided teachings about the behavior of the Holy Spirit have introduced confusion about who he is and how he works, and has negatively impacted the thinking of mankind. This negativity has also affected some believers and their willingness to truly worship him. True worship must involve man's spirit. True worship will also engage your emotions, and involve your recall of historical and contemporary thoughts, incidents, and challenges. Remember, God is a spirit and the entire conversation about God and godlessness is a spiritual conversation. So, without an intelligent appreciation of sound scriptural doctrine, humans cannot enter into true godly worship. God requires our worship of him, in spirit and in truth. He also requires a coherent approach to our worship. Believers should understand that if we pursue all truth or rigid doctrine to the exclusion of the spirit, who is often evidenced by the involvement of human emotions, this solely doctrinal course of action, will produce *"dead orthodoxy"*, or dead tradition. Dead orthodoxy or tradition will produce a church filled with unspiritual, competing, pretenders who will ask a spiritual God to produce spiritual results in their daily lives, while they remain aloof from all things spiritual. However, on the other hand, all spirit or all emotion without truth and doctrine produces empty excitement and strange behavior. This course of action cultivates a vibrant people who may reject the discipline of scriptural, godly conduct. With truth or doctrine alone, a church will dry up, diminishing in influence and attendance. Likewise, with Spirit or emotions alone, the church will blow up, will cease to exist, or become identified as a loose place where anything goes. But, when Spirit and truth are combined, the church will grow up and mature with influence as a stable and godly church. Spirit and truth together are what we seek, in our church and in our lives.

From Creation to the Present:

So we start at creation, the beginning of mankind, as we prepare to grasp the inexhaustible teaching of the Tabernacle of Moses in the Wilderness. Although it is not widely understood in Christendom, the tabernacle teaching is designed by God as a prerequisite to the current-day believer's understanding and full appreciation of salvation. It also enhances our grasp of all scripture, commonly known as the Holy Bible. The patterns of worship, sacrifice, and cleansing acceptable to God in the tabernacle, demonstrated how God intended to deal with sinful man, following man's original sin, in the Garden of Eden. And since God is the same yesterday, today, and forever, accuracy in our understanding requires a look back to examine the historical record from the creation of mankind.

Man's beginning with God takes us back to a time long ago, to a place called eternity; to a place where Jesus, the Holy Spirit, God the Father, and his created man were all in spirit form; it takes us back to that spiritual world which preceded the entrance of sin into the universe; to that place where God lives and where mankind used to live. In our search for truth and accuracy, we must think back to that original world prior to Romans 5:12, *"where by one man (Adam) sin entered into the world, and death by sin; and so death passed upon all men."* We go back to that place where mankind had never known or committed sin. But moving from then toward our current existence, we discover man's original sin in the Garden of Eden also addressed in the book of Romans. *"All mankind has sinned and fallen short of the glory (purpose) of God" (Romans 3:23)*. [All have missed the mark of innocence that God intended for the human race, for all eternity]. Because of the fall (original sin), mankind became separated from God, separated from the original state of man's creation.

However, God never lost sight of his original intent for mankind first mentioned in the book of Genesis: *"And God said, Let us make man in our image, after our likeness: and let them have dominion over the fish of the sea, and over the fowl of the air, and over the cattle, and over all the earth, and over every creeping thing that creepeth upon the earth" (Genesis 1:26)*.

His purpose regarding man is further clarified by the psalmist in Psalm 8:6: *"Thou madest him (mankind) to have dominion over the works of thy hands."* The ultimate duty of man is set forth in Ecclesiastes 12:13: *"Let us hear the conclusion of the whole matter: fear God, and keep his commandments: for this is the whole duty of man."* Since the fall of mankind, God always intended to redeem man from his sinful and powerless condition, and God's desire to have mankind superintend his universe was never diminished.

So, God himself instructed Moses to make him (God) a dwelling place on earth that he might come down and dwell among his people. One of the reasons God came to earth was to create and establish an acceptable way for sinful man to atone for his sins and return to God. In Leviticus 17:11, God, says: *"For the life of the flesh is in the blood: and I have given it to you upon the altar to make an atonement for your souls: for it is the blood that maketh an atonement for the soul."* Here, God reveals that life for every living creature is in the blood and that he has designated the blood for the atonement of the human soul (actually spirit). God soon gave instructions in this Old Testament Tabernacle of Moses to illustrate that the requirement for cleansing man from sin was the sacrificial shedding of the blood of a substitute on behalf of sinful man.

Here, in the tabernacle, this principle of substitutionary atonement is introduced as the way for sinful man to again qualify to carry out God's original plan; for man to have rule over all creation.

This substitutionary sacrificial system is the foundation which paves the way used by God to later send his Son Jesus Christ to die on Calvary's cross and make available salvation and restoration to all mankind; to regain their original qualification to have dominion and authority over the works of God's hands.

The father equips those who accept his Son Jesus to spiritually experience the "glory of God" here on earth. He also makes available faith and the anointing by his spirit; through the exercise of faith, believers gain access to God's anointing, and experience his presence. The exercise of faith and exposure to the anointing reawakens the sensation of what mankind experienced in the Garden of Eden when they walked with God in the cool of the evening. Whenever believers assemble together here on earth, it is God's purpose to draw them spiritually, emotionally, and supernaturally into his glory. *God's glory means to be immersed in total awareness of God's presence and purpose and to trust his fatherly oversight and supervision of our lives to the extent we enjoy a sense of yieldedness to the reality of his preeminence, authority, and influence.* Remember, in his presence is fullness of joy. As we look back in time to mankind's creation, we should examine what our Bible experience has taught us, and what we already know and accept from the historical record of scripture. Let us remind ourselves with a quick review of spiritual truth that many of us have previously learned.

Previously Gained Knowledge:

(1) The historical record of scripture has taught us that God created man: *"And God said, Let us make man in our image, after our likeness: and let them have dominion over the fish of the sea, and over the fowl of the air, and over the cattle, and over all the earth, and over every creeping thing that creepeth upon the earth" (Genesis 1:26).*

(2)   The historical record has taught us that man lived with God in eternity in the Garden of Eden called Paradise. *"And the Lord God formed man of the dust of the ground, and breathed into his nostrils the breath of life; and man became a living soul. And the Lord God planted a garden eastward in Eden; and there he put the man whom he had formed"* (Genesis 2:7–8). In the garden, it was the custom of God to walk with Adam in the cool of the evening. *"And they heard the voice of the Lord God walking in the garden in the cool of the day: and Adam and his wife hid themselves from the presence of the Lord God amongst the trees of the garden"* (Genesis 3:8).

(3)   The historical record of scripture has taught us that man enjoyed all the benefits of relationship with God. Adam was given the privilege of naming every living creature that God created. Also, the record shows that God gave Adam a helpmate in the Garden of Eden.

"And the Lord God said, it is not good that the man should be alone; I will make him an help meet for him. And out of the ground the Lord God formed every beast of the field and every fowl of the air; and brought them unto Adam to see what he would call them: and whatsoever Adam called every living creature that was the name thereof. And Adam gave names to all cattle, and to the fowl of the air and to every beast of the field; but for Adam there was not found an help meet for him. And the Lord God caused a deep sleep to fall upon Adam, and he slept: and he took one of his ribs, and closed up the flesh instead thereof; And the rib, which the Lord God had taken from man, made he a woman, and brought her unto the man. And Adam said this is now bone of my bones, and flesh of my flesh: she shall be called woman, because she was taken out of man. Therefore shall a man leave his father and his mother, and shall cleave unto his wife: and they shall be one flesh" (Genesis 2:18–24).

(4)	The historical record of scripture has taught us that Mankind disobeyed God: *"Now the serpent was more subtle than any beast of the field which the Lord God had made. And he said unto the woman, Yea, hath God said, Ye shall not eat of every tree of the garden? And the woman said unto the serpent, we may eat of the fruit of the trees of the garden: But of the fruit of the tree which is in the midst of the garden, God hath said, Ye shall not eat of it, neither shall ye touch it, lest ye die. And the serpent said unto the woman, Ye shall not surely die: For God doth know that in the day ye eat thereof, then your eyes shall be opened, and ye shall be as gods, knowing good and evil. And when the woman saw that the tree was good for food, and that it was pleasant to the eyes, and a tree to be desired to make one wise, she took of the fruit thereof, and did eat, and gave also unto her husband with her; and he did eat"* (Genesis 3:1–6).

(5)	The historical record of scripture has taught us that Man was barred from the Garden of Eden. For the first time, mankind enters the realm of time. Remember, God does not live in time; God lives in eternity. *"Therefore, the Lord God sent him forth from the Garden of Eden, to till the ground from whence he was taken. So he drove out the man; and he placed at the east of the garden of Eden Cherubim, and a flaming sword which turned every way, to keep the way of the tree of life"* (Genesis 3:23–24).

(6)	The historical record of scripture has taught us that all have sinned and come short of the glory of God. For some unexplained reason, mankind, beginning with Adam, has taken transgression of the commandments of God lightly. We read the Word of God, but somehow we find a way in our own reasoning, to exempt ourselves from the instructions found there. Deuteronomy says: *"Know therefore that the Lord thy God, he is God, the faithful God, which keepeth covenant and mercy with them that love him and keep his commandments to a thousand generations"* (Deuteronomy 7:9). Then see Romans 3:23, a divine message to man: "All mankind has missed the mark of innocence that God intended for man, from the foundation of the world." It means we have lost the benefits of the glory of our original creation. In addition to what the historical record has taught us, a closer look at the eighth division of Psalms will refresh and enrich our historical perspective regarding the position of humanity with God from ancient times. Psalm 8 is one of several psalms known as "creation hymns." Others in this group are Psalm 19:1–6, and Psalms 33 and 104 in their entirety.

Psalm 8.

What clarity of man's relationship with God is offered here as we look at the scriptural record in Psalm 8? *"O Lord, our Lord, how excellent is thy name in all the earth; who hast set thy glory above the heavens."* This first verse ties God's name and his glory together to demonstrate that from the beginning, God and his glory has filled all of creation. Verse 2 deals with mankind: *"Out of the mouth of babes and suckling's hast thou ordained strength because of thine enemies, that thou mightest still the enemy and the avenger."* God has ordained man, even in his most feeble and inarticulate state (babes or suckling infants), to overcome the most spiteful, malicious, or wicked enemies of God. Verses 3 and 4 draw a contrast between the vastness of creation and the perceived insignificance of the human creation. These verses raise the question in the mind of David, and those of his generation, of the value of man: *"When I consider thy heavens, the work of thy fingers, the moon and the stars, which thou hast ordained; what is man, that thou art mindful of him? And the son of man, that thou visitest him?"* What is man that God would pay attention to him?

In verses 5–8 we first see and understand that God's purpose for creating humanity is divine; man is created to rule over the works of God's hands. We also see that man's purpose is vast and significant;

God made mankind to be a little lower than angels and to rule over all creation: *"For thou hast made him a little lower than the angels and hast crowned him with glory and honor. Thou madest him to have dominion over the works of thy hands; thou hast put all things under his feet: All sheep and oxen, yea, and the beasts of the field; the fowl of the air, and the fish of the sea, and whatsoever passeth through the paths of the seas."*

And finally in verse 9, David, the king, statesman, and writer of psalms is as awestruck at the end as at the start of this psalm. Even though David's view of the vastness and significance of man's responsibility and of his divine nature, and his importance to God, had been made clear, David's appreciation for who God is was no less awesome. So, in verse 9, David repeats, *"O Lord, our Lord, how excellent is thy name in all the earth!"*

REVELATION VERSUS REASON

And now we examine a subject so critical to the peace, joy, and well being of humanity. It might be said that understanding these principles is the key to life here on earth. Mankind must be aware of and understand these two ancient, but opposing, principles if he is to truly walk in the peace and power that is his. If humans will understand and exercise this knowledge, life on earth becomes spirit-led and productive. When Revelation and Reason, two rarely taught, however, extremely essential ancient principles, are understood and employed, man's spiritual return to his original relationship with God is inevitable. A major obstacle to present-day humanity's ability to walk in wealth, prosperity, and peace on earth is his lack of knowledge regarding these two principles.

Much of the Western church overlooks or avoids this teaching. However, without an understanding of these foundational truths, well-meaning Christians will often find themselves bogged down and focusing on matters of minor importance, while ignoring the major teachings of scripture, which are essential to finding peace in spiritual relationship with God. The lack of understanding regarding revelation versus reason also contributes to the weakness of the modern church. The scriptures say, *"My people are destroyed for a lack of knowledge"* (*Hosea 4:6*). So, it is key that believers study these principles to comprehend the difference between the character and power of revelation, versus the character and power of reason.

Here in the Western world, too many people, both in and out of the church, have not considered how mankind regressed from his original position and favor with God at creation (where we enjoyed unimpeded access to whatever man desired), to the present place of struggle for basic needs. Too many of us, especially believers, have failed to ask ourselves how and why humanity has moved from living in the very presence and continuous communing with God, to a place where, when we gather or assemble to meet with God in our churches, too often the services are powerless, predictable, and uninspiring. How can it be that those who come to accept the God we offer continue to live as though the God of the scriptures does not exist? How can it be that congregants come to the altar seeking help for their life situation and come back next week seeking help for the same situation? Is it that we serve an ineffectual God? Or could it be that the doctrine of man has such an influence in our appeal that the doctrine of God has no effect in our lives and the lives of the congregants? Could it be that we need to change our approach? Or is it just that our God is impotent?

Now, while we all see through a glass darkly (1 Corinthians 13:12), and no human being can claim to have the all-encompassing solution or answer to the needs of mankind (nor the needs of God's church), God loves humanity much too much to deny us a spiritual solution to any problem or circumstance that plagues us, or that offends him. He told us in Psalm 8 that even as babes and sucklings; we are empowered to overcome any enemy of ours, or his. Our Lord, Jesus Christ, aware of our needs present and future, upon departing the earth sent the Holy Spirit, whose assignment is to lead us, teach us, and guide us into all truth. *"Howbeit when he, the Spirit of truth, is come, he will guide you into all truth: for he shall not speak of himself; but whatsoever he shall hear, that shall he speak: and he will shew you things to come"* (*John 16:13*). Also see

John 14:26 *"But the comforter, which is the holy ghost, whom the father will send in my name, he shall teach you all things, and bring all things to your remembrance, whatsoever I have said unto you."* God has provided a leader, a teacher, and one sent to guide all mankind here on earth. However, he speaks through spiritual revelation of the scriptures and, as we embrace the revelation of Old and New Testament scriptures, we will hear his voice more clearly.

Too often the approach of the Western church to the scriptures has lacked organization. Little effort is made to take into account the broad scope and connections between the main scriptural focus and other supporting Bible scriptures. As a result, Christendom's learning habits have become choppy and fragmented. The result of this fragmentation is that the broad, all-encompassing picture painted by scripture is muddled. True Bible learning, like our approach to life itself, is more productive when we plan our approach and move progressively through the plan.

As we think about the differences in the character and power of the principle of revelation, and the character and power of the principle of reason, we are reminded that in eternity, original man's capacity to know anything apart from God was nonexistent. He knew only what was revealed or spoken to him by God; that's revelation. In fact, all that he knew was God. The oxygen of original man's world was the glory of God. Mankind, in original spirit form, ate, slept, and breathed God.

Today the human spirit recognizes there is a missing element, a void, in our current-day existence; and our human spirit desires to recapture the original relationship we had with God before the fall of man. The human *spirit* is in search of that relationship; however, *the conscious or soulish mind of man,* is not sure what is missing and often attempts to fill that felt-void with all the wrong things or all the wrong people. Originally, we lived in constant contact and relationship with the very presence of God, *the I AM,* and our spirit hungers to go back to that place; and because of the work of Christ on the cross, man is permitted to return to that relationship. However, it is a spiritual experience that is the most authentic and powerful influence on earth. The return to this relationship with God requires man's recognition, acceptance, and yielded submission to God in all of who He is as Elohim, God the I AM, God the Father-Son-and-Holy-Ghost, as Adonai, and as El-Shaddai.

The person who truly desires to walk with God and pursue spiritual revelation will seek God as Elohim, meaning God in Plurality, manifold, majestic, and magnificent ruler, as Father, Son and Holy Spirit, as God who was, and is, and is to come. He is Adonai, our creator and master. He is El-Shaddai, God almighty, able to bless all mankind, with all manner of blessings and He is God, the I Am, able to do whatever you need.

Those who have truly decided to walk with God, will embrace his spirit, and through the guidance of the spirit seek God's revealed knowledge, his revelation as supreme to all else, including human reason.

Originally created man could truly say, *"In him [God] we live and move and have our being" (Acts 17:28)*. Before the fall (original sin) mankind did not know he was naked; he did not know disease, or illness, or age, or sin; he didn't know time or future. He knew only God, in his ultimate all-encompassing, self-sufficient power, God, the I Am. They truly did live in the presence and glory of God.

We learn in Genesis 1:1 that *"In the beginning God created the heaven and the earth,"* and in Genesis 1:26, we see that God created man. Further, in Genesis 2:7 we see that God breathed into man's nostrils the breath of life and man became a living, breathing, speaking being. This Genesis 2:7 language is a *translation* rather than an *interpretation* of the original Hebrew text. The original Hebraic writings would have said either of the following: *(1) God imparted himself to man. Or (2) like God, did God make man, and man became a living, breathing, speaking being.* Remember, the original scriptures came out of the spirit of God; they were breathed by God himself and written down by chosen men for all mankind to live by. *"All scripture is given by inspiration of God, and is profitable for doctrine, for reproof, for correction, for instruction in righteousness" 2 Tim. 3:16.* The book of James instructs us to be doers of the word and not hearers only. The scriptures are given by God, to mankind as instructions to live by and to shape our life here on earth to fit within his love. However, Westerners must remember, these original writings were given to the Hebrew-speaking people of the middle eastern region of the world, to people of the Hebraic culture. So these original writings were translated with the Hebrew mind-set. Also, it is helpful to remember that in biblical days the scriptures referred to two classes of people: the *Jews* and the *Gentiles.* This word *Gentile* is a Latin term used by some translators to refer to non-Israeli people or nations.

Those who were not born into the Hebrew or Jewish culture were identified as Gentiles. Non-Hebrews called Gentiles came mainly from the Greek culture and the Greeks were known as great thinkers. Many respected thinkers and philosophers were of the Greek culture and they applied strong human reasoning to all matters of consideration including the scriptures. Thinkers became popular as the wise and intelligent class, and men who considered themselves and/or were considered by others as great thinkers, introduced the world to *the age of reason.* Accordingly, many Westerners, being non-Hebrew, have a Gentile heritage. We were raised and educated in the Western culture; our early modern universities were modeled after the academy of Plato, a Greek philosopher. Our Greco-Roman, Western mind-set causes us to struggle with prehistoric linguistic and cultural concepts and implications, found in scripture. Our own human reasoning can be, and often is, a hindrance to our achieving a true spiritual grasp of the meaning of ancient middle-eastern historical writings.

Westerners are reading a Bible given to us through a Middle

Eastern culture and mind-set; and at best we sometimes, struggle with understanding the original meaning of the scripture text. Scholars tell us that the Greek mind relates things more to function than to form. Many words that have the same sound and the same spelling in English, can and often do, have a very different meaning in the Hebrew or Greek languages. One example of this is the word "conversation". In English it means to have a talk or discussion with another person. However, in Greek it can mean "life style". In the Hebraic culture, meanings are heavily influenced by function and by the scriptures, or by how the Jewish culture perceives the intent of the mind of God. Most often, the sense or understanding in the Hebrew culture is not so much *I have figured this thing out; instead, it is God has revealed this thing to me.* Upon reviewing these two cultures, it is easy to understand that, because the Greek culture has a heavy influence in the Western world, truth is often based on the natural senses, of seeing, hearing, and thinking. In Western culture, *truth* is heavily influenced by intellectualism or human reasoning. The Greek or Western mind-set would say, "*Seeing is believing,*" while the Hebrew mind-set would say, "*To believe is to see.*"

Only God, by his Spirit, is capable of producing revelation, while reasoning comes from the human mind. Revelation may very well be inspired by words or actions of a human being, but true revelation does not originate in the mind of man; revelation is from God. As we discuss this question of reasoning versus revelation, some Bible readers will remember Isaiah 1:18–19 where God says, "*Come now, let us reason together.*" Many have interpreted this scripture as Father God issuing an invitation for humans to bargain or negotiate with him. No. God is calling the nation of Israel to repentance. He is presenting the nation with two options: (1) repent and enjoy the fat (prosperity) of the land, or (2) continue in your rebellious ways and face destruction.

The inevitable questions raised by this discussion then become: How did mankind descend from the realm of revelation, where he was created and lived for a time, to the realm of reason? How did mankind fall from the glory of God in eternity? How did we end up living in the realm of time? Mankind arrived at this new place as a result of his choice to sin. Man's original sin occurred in the Garden of Eden; however, the fall continues to occur whenever a human decides to obey a voice other than the voice of God, and whenever a human takes the rebellious step of transgression in violation of the father's instructions. God's instructions in the Garden of Eden were not to eat from the *Tree of the Knowledge of Good and Evil.* Mankind disobeyed; it was that single rebellious act, to partake of the **Tree of Knowledge** that enabled humans to reason. Satan had said *if you eat, you will not die.* To the reasoning mind it may have appeared that Satan was right. Adam and Eve ate of the forbidden tree and yet they lived for many years. However, in the spiritual kingdom it is understood that God spoke of a spiritual death, which occurred immediately. But carnal minded man was then, and is today, unable to understand the spiritual. So mankind might have thought, *what else might we get away with?* That's reasoning.

Because Adam and Eve's disobedience was a willful act of sin, it removed humankind from the protection and faithfulness of God that they enjoyed under his covering from creation. Since Adam and Eve's eviction from the Garden, humanity's thinking has been halted between two opinions. In the book of 1 Kings 18:21, the choice was between God and Baal. However, now the choice is between God's revealed instructions and human reasoning. The choice is to adhere to revelation from God, or to adhere to reasoning produced by the mind of Man. There are still times when we should and must use our ability to reason. Should I drive or ride the bus to work? Should I eat an old-fashioned fat-filled, high-cholesterol meal, or should I eat a healthy meal? These and many other life questions will require reasoning. But when the choice is between what God says as opposed to what human reasoning concludes, remember you are making a choice between righteousness, peace, joy, and prosperity on the one hand, and present-day torment, and devastation on the other.

The rebellious act we have been referring to known in scripture as the fall (original sin) alienated man from *"God, the I Am,"* in whom we lived, moved, and had our being, to the place where we acquired the ability to think separate and apart from God. That rebelliousness moved us into the age of human reason.

With the fall, mankind began to know time, and with the knowledge of time came the knowledge of the future. As we gained the ability to anticipate the future, we came to know death in all its forms: spiritual, emotional, and mental death. The mental death, suffered by humanity at the fall, causes the average human today to use less than five (5) percent of the brain capacity given him by God.

When people live and walk out their life guided by the principle of reason, it is impossible to fully embrace the principle of revelation. In other words, where reason rules, revelation finds little, if any, acceptance. The opposite is also true: where the principle of spiritual revelation rules, the principle of reason vacates.

There is scripture that explains this phenomenon in 1 Corinthians: *"which things also we speak, not in the words which man's wisdom teacheth, but which the Holy Ghost teacheth; comparing spiritual things with spiritual. But the natural man receiveth not the things of the Spirit of God: for they are foolishness unto him: neither can he know them, because they are spiritually discerned"* (1 Corinthians 2:13-14).

If one thinks about it, everything they receive from God is spiritually granted, and every time one feels close to God, it is spiritually detected. Each time one truly connects with God in prayer, natural thoughts must be cleared from the mind, and spiritually you sense his presence and speak directly to him. When this happens, you do not *think*, you *know* he heard your prayer. Many believers become skeptical or leery at the mention of spiritual activity. With just a little thought, they would know that God is not natural; He is spiritual and all things godly are spiritual. No natural thing or person can touch any aspect of God. If we will just use the brain that God gave us, we will understand that man is natural; God is supernatural. In Mark 8:34 we read: *"And when he [Jesus] had called the people unto him with his disciples also, he said unto them, whosoever will come after me, let him deny himself, and take up his cross, and follow me."* Also, 1 Corinthians 2:13-14 is so powerful that it seems that even a wayfaring person, let alone a believer, would grasp it. *"Which things also we speak, not in the words which man's wisdom teacheth, but which the Holy Ghost teacheth; comparing spiritual things with spiritual. But the natural man receiveth not the things of the Spirit of God: for they are foolishness unto him: neither can he know them, because they are spiritually discerned. 1 Corinthians 2:13-14.* See:

"And an highway shall be there, and a way, and it shall be called The way of holiness; the unclean shall not pass over it; but it shall be for those: the wayfaring men, though fools, shall not err therein Isaiah 35:8.

The Western mind is not readily amenable to the idea of denying itself. For the most part, its level of commitment to follow anything or anyone is based entirely on its ability to reason as to why it should follow that course of action. The Western mind generally does not recognize the need to see God from an evolving perspective; that he is first Elohim, God spiritually with us, in plurality and majesty, who made us and who requires our submitting to him. Westerners appear not to understand that as we submit to God's way, he is more fully revealed to us until we finally know him as more than enough, as whatever we need, as the unlimited all-sufficient "God the I AM."

Our Western mind-set and our preference for reasoning over revelation blurs our ability to see God's Word clearly and places us dangerously close to a group that the apostle Paul referred to in 2 Corinthians 4:3–4: *"But if our gospel be hid, it is hid to them that are lost: In whom the god of this world (Satan) hath blinded the minds of them which believe not, lest the light of the glorious gospel of Christ, who is the image of God, should shine unto them."*

When we search for what is both attractive and powerful enough to prevent mankind from accepting and acting on God's revelation, we find it is a "reason."

While professed believers are halted between obeying their mind and following God's instructions, far too many people who sit in the pews of the Western church, known as the body of Christ, are hurting deeply. They are living in need of deliverance, restoration, clear teaching, and many are dying much too early. This is because we teach them to have faith in their own reasoning power, as opposed to placing their faith in the principles and commandments of God's revealed word. When they come to the altar in our churches, we stand in their presence and offer a general prayer, as opposed to equipping ourselves and laying our anointed hands on them and ministering to whatever hurt or need they bring. Where there is little faith in revelation, there will also be little peace of mind, joy, and prosperity. God is calling all mankind and especially His church to maturity, to accept the scriptural responsibility of Philippians 2, to work out their your soul salvation, *"Wherefore, my beloved, as ye have always obeyed, not as in my presence only, but now much more in my absence, work out your own salvation with fear and trembling"* (*Philippians 2:12*). God's church has been given the power and authority to set at liberty the captives of this and the next generation. It is always God's plan that we take responsibility for our current generation and prepare the way for the next generation and beyond.

The Power of Faith

Hebrews 11:6 gives these instructions: *"But without faith it is impossible to please him: for he that cometh to God must believe that he is [exists] and that he is a rewarder of them that diligently seek him."* This verse describes the requirement to move beyond reading His word to searching for meaning often only found in the original language. We must cultivate the tradition of studying his Word with all diligence. The verse also describes the deep level of conviction and the unwavering attitude that undergirds true faith in God's love and His willingness to work on your behalf. First, we must believe that God exists as our infinite and prevailing father, who loves and cares for us personally. We must believe that God will respond to our diligence, and hear us when we pray. We must know that God is more than willing to be our refuge (sanctuary, safe haven, and strength), that he wants to be my very present help in my times of trouble. The power of the reasoning mind sets a cap, a limit on faith. This cap, or ceiling, is most often born out of the mind's inability or unwillingness to deny itself, to crucify self-indulgent passions, and chose to follow God. The maturity of faith comes by hearing the Word of God and embracing God's instructions on a matter. The ingredient for igniting the power of faith in our lives is deposited in the persuasive revelation of God's Word. Maturity of faith will manifest in a person's life when their personal commitment to follow God's instructions becomes strong enough to bypass the reasoning influence of their mind and they embrace the revelation of God.

Power of the Anointing

If believing Christine leaders, functioning under the power of the anointing of the Holy Spirit, will preach and teach from the scriptures about *Jesus Christ as Lord and Savior,* a majority of the hearers, by the spirit of God, will receive the revelation that Jesus Christ is Lord and Savior. That revelation will ignite the spark of faith that anoints *(empowers)* the congregant's belief system or the mind *(different from the brain),* that Jesus Christ is Lord and Savior, and the congregants are then able to embrace Jesus Christ as their personal Lord and Savior.

Likewise, if believing leaders, under the anointing of the Holy Spirit, will preach and teach the scriptures on healing and deliverance, the congregants will, *by the spirit of God,* receive the revelation that healing and deliverance is God's will for their lives. Revelation will ignite the spark of faith that anoints *(empowers)* the congregant's belief system or the mind *(different from the brain),* to embrace and receive their healing and deliverance from so many satanic woes in their lives. Further, if believing leaders, under the anointing, will teach what the scriptures say about the tithe and offerings, the hearers, *by the anointing of the spirit of God,* will receive the revelation on giving and will embrace biblical giving: *"The entrance of thy word giveth light; it giveth understanding to the simple Psalm 119:130."* If believer/leaders fail to teach on these and other matters by the anointing of the spirit, then they do a disservice to their congregation: *"For what is it wherein ye were inferior to other churches, except it be that I myself was not burdensome to you? Forgive me this wrong, 2 Corinthians 12:13."* As leaders must remember that it is God who works through us to produce effectiveness in kingdom work. Believers are insufficient of themselves, but by his spirit we are unstoppable. *"Not that we are sufficient of ourselves to think anything as of ourselves; but our sufficiency is of God; Who also hath made us able ministers of the new testament; not of the letter, but of the spirit: for the letter killeth, but the spirit giveth life"* (2 Corinthians 3:5-6). Finally, *"My people are destroyed for a lack of knowledge"* (Hosea 4:6).

Jesus Christ:
Starting at the Beginning

Shortly following *the Passion of Christ* (used here, to mean the story of the arrest, trial, crucifixion, burial and resurrection of Jesus), He, being the master of all teachers, provides an example of *starting at the beginning* as He taught spiritual truth to two of his followers. To witness this teaching, we go back in our minds to the year AD 33, to the city of Jerusalem.

The scene opens on the third day following his death, burial, and resurrection. It appears that Jesus is gone forever; also, many strange and unusual events have occurred over the past three days. The whole earth, which just three days earlier was in darkness from the sixth to the ninth hour, is still in shock and people are not quite sure what they have just witnessed. They are unsettled about the meaning of these unfamiliar events and everything is hushed. The birds are respectfully quiet, even the trees are stilled; the wind refrains from movement; the animals are muted and appear to be in wonderment; even nature seems in a hushed perplexity.

Against this background, you and I begin our mental journey back into the annals of time. We find ourselves on an ancient, hot, and dusty road between Jerusalem and a little known city named Emmaus. It is here that we encounter two tired and puzzled disciples of Jesus Christ as they are walking toward the city of Emmaus. Luke 24:13-14, referring to these two men, says this: *"and, behold, two of them [disciples] went that same day to a village called Emmaus, which was from Jerusalem about threescore furlongs. And they talked together of all these things which had happened"*.

An obvious question is *what things?* What did they talk about? A review of the historical, scriptural proceedings for those three days reveals several events they could have discussed: Why was it that between the hours of nine o'clock in the morning and noon, as Jesus hung dying on the cross, he spoke a word of forgiveness? *"Father, forgive them for they know not what they do?"* (Luke 23:34) Or, why during that same time period, our Lord Jesus, immobilized death long enough to grant salvation to the repentant thief there on a cross beside him? Saying: *"This day shall you be with me in paradise?"*(Luke 23:43). Or, why he spoke a word of love, care, and responsibility when he said to his own mother Mary, *"Woman, behold thy son,"*and to the beloved disciple John, he said, *"Behold thy mother?"* (*John 19:26–27*).

They may have talked of how from noon to three p.m., darkness covered the whole earth; and during this time period, the Lord refrained from speaking, but at the ninth hour, 3:00 p.m., he spoke a word of spiritual distress as he let out a loud shout in the Greek language, *"Eloi, Eloi, Lama Sabachthani?"* That is to say, *"My God, my God, why hast thou forsaken me?"* (*Mark 15:34*). And at John 19:28, scripture tells us He spoke a word of physical agony saying simply, *"I thirst."* Then he speaks a word of triumph when he declares, *"It is finished"* (*John 19:30*). Finally, he speaks a word in his native Aramaic langue of total trust and devotion when he says: *"Father, into thy hands I commit my spirit"* (*Luke 23:46*).

While scripture does not give us exact details of what these two men talked about. The scriptures, in the book of Luke pick up the narrative and make the important point of this section as it reveals that without their knowledge of his presence, Jesus had been walking with these two disciples and listening to their conversation; as finally he appears to them and asks several questions. At first Cleopas asks him, "Are you a stranger unaware of the recent things that have happened here?" Then Jesus asks, *"What things?"* Luke writes: *"And he said unto them, 'What things?' "But their eyes were holden that they should not know him. And he said unto them, 'What manner of communications are these that ye have one to another, as ye walk, and are sad?' And the one of them, whose name was Cleopas, answering said unto him, 'Art thou only a stranger in Jerusalem, and hast not known the things which are come to pass there in these days?' And he said unto them, 'What things?' And they said unto him, 'Concerning Jesus of Nazareth, which was a prophet mighty in deed and word before God and all the people: And how the chief priests and our rulers delivered him to be condemned to death, and have crucified him. But we trusted that it had been he which should have redeemed Israel: and beside all this, today is the third day since these things were done"* (Luke 24:16–21).

Then Jesus revealed himself to these disciples at Luke 24:25 and immediately rebuked them because they had not believed the things that Moses and all the prophets had preached and prophesied for many years. The Old Testament prophets continually taught the coming of Messiah. So, Jesus said to them: *"O fools, and slow of heart to believe all that the prophets have spoken."* In verse 26, he says: *"Ought not Christ to have suffered these things, and to enter into his glory?"* In other words, did not the prophets of old, prophesy that the messiah would come, did you not believed them? And why shouldn't Jesus be the one and assume the glory of the messiahship; and then he taught them, as verse Luke 24: 27 says, *"And beginning at Moses and all the prophets, he expounded unto them in all the scriptures the things concerning himself."*

Later, Cleopas and his unnamed friend were asked how the Lord had joined them, and they did not have an answer. At first they thought he had stepped out of the shadows, but they just were not sure where he had come from. Notice that though they were unsure about many things, they were very sure and had clear articulation about one thing: that Jesus had taken the ancient scriptures, the Torah, the first five books of the Bible (which was all the Bible available at the time), and starting at the very beginning, Jesus Christ had explained the scriptures in a way that made remarkable sense. The clarity of his teaching had driven from their minds all confusion, bewilderment, frustration, and doubt. And now, they were elated and encouraged by their new understanding of God's Word.

Just as you and I and every living human being need to hear the message of the gospel of Jesus Christ and the salvation he offers, Cleopas and his friend also, needed to hear the gospel of Jesus Christ. And just as Jesus started at the beginning of the Old Testament historical record and explained the scriptures as he taught them with unmistakable clarity, now let us together, writer and reader, start at the beginning and carefully study our way through the scriptures as we examine the Old Testament teaching of the Tabernacle of Moses in the Sinai wilderness.

The Examination of the Tabernacle of Moses

The scriptures reveal profound, irrefutable lessons about life, death, heaven, hell, and all God has created. So, if one considers oneself to be educated or even well informed, one must have at least a foundational understanding of the Holy Scriptures. Further, no human being can have real peace of mind without a basic knowledge of God's Word. I believe it is also true that one cannot truly understand salvation, without a minimal knowledge of what the Tabernacle of Moses is about.

The scriptures are filled with the richness and depth of the glory of our creator, richness and depth that go well beyond our human comprehension. We read about our God and we are awestruck by his continuous insertion of divine intervention on behalf of those who live by his precepts. I have worked to lay a foundation, for our understanding of this Old Testament Tabernacle and how it relates to salvation for the modern-day believer. I am comfortable that a sufficient foundation has been laid.

The Tabernacle on earth happened because God decided to dwell on earth among His people. So, God instructed Moses to build this tabernacle on earth. However, God in his wisdom, instructed Moses to explain to the people the plan to construct the tabernacle. It would be through their giving, from the spoils they brought out of Egypt, their labor, and other contributions that the tabernacle would be built. Throughout history this pattern has been repeated and followed: when a new sanctuary is to be built for worship and service to the Most High God, repeatedly the people of God have brought their offerings, their gifts, their talents, and labor to build or restore God's house. *"And the Lord spake unto Moses, saying, speak unto the children of Israel, that they bring me an offering: of every man that giveth it willingly with his heart ye shall take my offering. And this is the offering which ye shall take of them; gold, and silver, and brass, And blue, and purple, and scarlet, and fine linen, and goats' hair, And rams' skins dyed red, and badgers' skins, and shittim wood, Oil for the light, spices for anointing oil, and for sweet incense, Onyx stones, and stones to be set in the ephod, and in the breastplate. And let them make me a sanctuary; that I may dwell among them. According to all that I shewed thee, after the pattern of the tabernacle, and the pattern of all the instruments thereof, even so shall ye make it"* Exodus 25:1–9. And Moses shared God's instructions with the people (see *Exodus 35:1–10);* and the people had to be restrained from giving offerings (see *Exodus 36:1–7).*

Scripture reminds us that God is the same yesterday, today, and forever. While the Israelites were wandering in the desert/wilderness, God showed himself to be loving, merciful, compassionate, and forgiving, even to a rebellious people, much like he does, for the church today.

As we study the instruments, people, ceremonies, and lessons of the tabernacle, continue to think back in time; allow yourself to mentally, emotionally, and spiritually experience the feelings of a people from long, long ago; walk where they walked; hear the sounds that they heard; smell what they smelled; and imagine being in that place. This spiritual experience will reconnect you and prepare you for our journey into, and the requirement to stand upon, holy ground. It will prepare you to embrace the newly revealed knowledge as we explore mysteries before hidden; and it could well, prepare you to live out the remainder of life here on earth, walking, living, and breathing in lockstep with God our father as you present yourself a living sacrifice to your maker.

God gave Moses the pattern of the tabernacle because He wanted to spend time among his people on earth and reveal eternal truths, including the requirements necessary and acceptable to him for sinful man's atonement. It is my prayer that this tabernacle study will lead you to a deeper understanding of the role the Old Tabernacle ceremonies played in preparing the way for current-day believer's salvation and lead you to a deeper and better understood relationship with Jesus Christ.

IMPORTANT EXPLANATIONS

The Tabernacle teaching contains unique, fundamental, and instructive subject matter. The following explanations should provide a basis for a richer understanding as we proceed.

The Tabernacle on earth was the Old Testament place where animal sacrifices were offered to God to atone for the sin of man; where the bread-of-presence, called the shewbread, was placed weekly before God's presence; where the incense was burned at the altar of incense; and where the menorah was lit daily and provided light for the *Holy Place*. The Tabernacle was also the place where the people gathered for Israel's three major annual feasts and for special occasions. *"Three times in a year shall all thy males appear before the Lord thy God in the place which he shall choose; in the **feast of unleavened bread**, and in the **feast of weeks**, and in the **feast of tabernacles**: and they shall not appear before the Lord empty" Deuteronomy 16:16.* The Tabernacle was not a synagogue; it was not designed, or intended to hold the entire *assembly of Israel* within its courts. *It was God's dwelling place on earth among his people, not the people's house.*

The Future Temple of Jerusalem

As they journeyed through the wilderness, God gave the Israelites instructions that when they came into the Promised Land and were settled there, they would build him a permanent structure. This instruction was a reference to Solomon's Temple (see *Deuteronomy 12:10-11)*. The tabernacle was the forerunner of Solomon's Temple. The Tabernacle, this tent in the Sinai wilderness, is the place where God's Shekinah glory, the visible, overwhelming, manifestation of God's presence, dwelt among the Israelites during the time of their wilderness experience from about 1400 BC until King Solomon built the temple in about 950 BC.

Names of the Tabernacle

In scripture, the Tabernacle is often referred to by different names. Some are as follows: It was called: *"the Sanctuary"*: emphasizing that this was holy space (*Exodus. 25:8)*; "*The Tabernacle*": from the Hebrew word meaning, to dwell, emphasizing God's dwelling on earth (*Exodus. 25:9); "The Tent"*: emphasizing the temporary nature of the dwelling (*Exodus. 26:36); "The Tabernacle of the congregation"*: emphasizing that this is where the people of the congregation met with God for purposes other than regular worship (*Exodus. 29:42);* and it was called *"the Tabernacle of the testimony":* Testimony is a name for the tablets of the Ten Commandments stored in the ark of the covenant located inside the tabernacle's holy of holies, emphasizing God's Law (*Exodus 38:21).*

The Horns of the Altar

The Israelites were commanded by God to use two altars in tabernacle worship. One was called the altar of burnt offering. It stood just inside the entrance to the tabernacle grounds and was overlaid with bronze ("brass"). The other was the altar of incense located inside the first section of the tabernacle-structure just in front of the veil that divided the holy place and the holy of holies. This altar was overlaid with gold. Both altars had four horns on their four corners and atonement was made on the horns of both altars. In some instances, if a man who had committed a trespass worthy of death could reach the horns of the altar, he could be protected from punishment. However, his protection depended on the intent of his heart at the time of the offense.

The Tabernacle and the Cross

Any mention of the Tabernacle of Moses evokes thoughts of symbolism; and yes, there are considerable symbols here, i.e., types and foreshadowing that are of major significance for New Testament readers. However, correct interpretation of the tabernacle's many lessons is only available by understanding the true meaning of the scriptures that describe the tabernacle. When we interpret meaning from the tabernacle story based on scripture, culture, and times of the events involved, we will understand the death, burial, and resurrection of Jesus Christ as a fulfillment of these Old Testament acts of atonement that came before in the tabernacle. There is nothing spooky about this approach.

The important facts regarding the tabernacle and the culture of that day are evident throughout the scriptures; this tabernacle, that was the dwelling place of God on earth, demonstrated major themes of the Bible, such as atonement, holiness, purification, sanctification, sacrifice, substitutionary-atonement for sin, and finally salvation. These themes come from scripture text, not from human imagination. The irresistible message of the tabernacle is this: God cannot be approached on human terms; one must offer a sacrifice and be cleansed to appear before the holiness of God. *In fact, entering God's holiness without the covering blood of Jesus would be fatal to sinful man.* God's presence dwelled within the inner chamber of the tabernacle, the Most Holy Place, and God received an audience with human flesh into his presence only once a year in the person of the high priest of Israel, who came bearing the blood-sacrifices for the people of the nation.

As our study takes us progressively through the Tabernacle, we move from the "outer court gate" toward the inner chamber where God's presence dwells. As we proceed along this path, we notice that the closer we move toward the place where God dwelled, the fewer the number of humans who enter upon this path. The outer courtyard is available to the entire congregation of Israel, but inside the first compartment of the tent (structure), called the Holy Place, only the priests (Aaron and his sons) in performance of their duty could enter; and, into the Holy of Holies, only one human, the high priest could enter. The concepts of purity abounded in the tabernacle. Priests were required to wash (be cleansed) before entering the holy spaces of the tabernacle. The purity laws of Israel had to do with God's holiness and man's requirement for holiness before God. They express how God separated himself from the laws of *sin and death.* He was then, and is now, the God of *righteousness, holiness, and everlasting life*; and he admonishes us to be like him. *"For I am the Lord your God: ye shall therefore sanctify yourselves, and ye shall be holy; for I am holy: neither shall ye defile yourselves with any manner of creeping thing that creepeth upon the earth."*

In the tabernacle, the sacrificial blood was splashed on the altar and on the walls of the sanctuary. However, we must understand that the shedding of the blood of the Messiah accomplishes much more than purification of man-made altars or the dashing of blood on the walls of the a man-made sanctuary. His blood was shed for purification of the confessing, repenting believer, who has now become God's sanctuary, his dwelling place on earth. *"The law of the spirit of life in Christ Jesus has made me free from the law of sin and death" (Romans 8:2).* The sanctification needed by every human being is now available because of the sacrificial blood of Jesus; and it was in the tabernacle, that God demonstrated the pattern that established the way for sinful man to return to his presence. That pattern for atonement in the tabernacle is a foreshadowing of the process to be used for the coming of Jesus Christ and the shedding of his blood at Calvary. The shedding of the blood of the animal substitute was replaced by the shedding of the blood of Jesus, our substitute Lamb of God, who came to redeem all humanity from Sin. The idea that sinful man without purification is unacceptable in God's direct presence flows throughout scriptures from Genesis through Revelation.

Finally, mankind must understand and accept that God made us in his image, to live forever in His presence, have relationship with him, and have rule over his creation. He makes this remarkably clear in the language of Psalms 8.

THE HIGH PRIEST

Aaron, the brother of Moses, was Israel's first high priest. He was later succeeded by his eldest surviving son, Eleazar. The position of high priest was the most prominent position in the Israelite hierarchy. The kings would often seek his counsel asking, *"Is there a word from the Lord?"* before engaging another nation in battle. The high priest wore special garments, including a turban or mitre, with a gold plate at its base. Some incorrectly call this turban a crown. He also wore a breastplate that contained the Urim and the Thummim (*Exodus 28:30).* He was allowed by God the privilege to minister in the holy of holies once a year during the Day of Atonement (around mid-September on our current calendar). The Day of Atonement is the holiest day of the year for the Jewish people. Its central themes are repentance and atonement. The day of atonement was then, and still is today, celebrated to bring about reconciliation between the people one to another, and between the individual and God. So the high priest was allowed into the Holy of Holies once every year to make atonement for his own sin, for the sins of all who lived in his household, and for the sins of the nation. Aaron as high priest is often called a type of Christ. His duties, his clothing, and his ministry were all a type and foreshadowing of our messianic liberator, Jesus Christ.

Today the shadow has been replaced by the real, by the authentic. Jesus Christ came to earth more than two thousand years ago as the high priest of good things to come by a greater and more perfect tabernacle not made with hands, that is, not of this creation. And he came not with the blood of goats and calves, but with his own blood he entered the authentic most Holy Place, heaven. And that he did only once for all; he entered and obtained eternal redemption from sin for any who will receive him. (To gain a better understanding read *Hebrews 9:11–14*).

The Tabernacle Furniture, Instruments and Materials

The Brazen Altar of Sacrifice:

The brazen altar of sacrifice was the place where the fire of God was maintained. It is the place where innocent animal-substitutes were sacrificed. Here, their blood was gathered and their portions were burned on the altar (see *Leviticus 6:5–6, 12,* and *Hebrews 9:22–24).* This altar represents the need for sacrifice before approaching God's presence, even for worship.

The Basin/Laver:

The laver in the old atonement system is where the priests wash their hands and feet before entering the tabernacle structure and before ministry at the brazen altar of sacrifice. Cleanliness is always required before entering either the service or the presence of the Most High God. This washing of hands and feet shows that cleansing is needed when any person wishes to draw nearer to God.

The Bread of Presence/Shewbread:

The bread of presence or shewbread was twelve loaves of bread: one to represent each of the twelve tribes of Israel. Also, there was oil and wine placed alongside the bread on the same table; some think the oil has reference to the Holy Spirit. These were daily kept before God's presence and refreshed weekly as a memorial, remembering God's provisions to Israel of grain, oil, and produce. Unlike other nations, Israel made no pretense that their God ate the bread, or needed food at all, but the table served as Israel's perpetual thanksgiving to God.

Menorah/Lampstand:

The menorah has seven branches, which represent the seven days of God's creation, and God's number of completion. The menorah gave light, and light is always present when we see God's glory in scripture. While God's glory illuminated the Holy of Holies, the light of the menorah was a symbol of the light of that glory located inside the initial room of the tent to give light in the Holy Place.

The Incense:

In the scriptures, God's glory [His visible overpowering presence] is always hidden with a cloud, even for the high priest. Seeing God's glory directly could be fatal (see *Leviticus 16:8–13*, with focus on *V:13*) *"And he shall put the incense upon the fire before the Lord, that the cloud of the incense may cover the mercy seat that is upon the testimony, that he die not."* The smoke-cloud from the burning incense preceded the high priest into the Holy of Holies or he would die. Normally, the incense was in the outer room, the Holy Place, just before the veiled-entrance into the holy of holies; however, upon entering into the presence of God, the high priest burned incense to create a cloud that shielded his humanity from the brightness of the glory of God.

The Ark of the Covenant:

The Ark of the Covenant was a square box with golden statues of cherubim (angels) attached to its lid. These cherubim represent God's throne and his footstool. Cherubim are heavenly beings that guard the presence and holiness of God. These are the same angles that guarded the gates to the Garden of Eden following the fall (original sin) of mankind.

Acacia Wood:

The Acacia wood sometimes called shittim wood is said to represent the incorruptible humanity referred to when Jesus Christ is called *the son of man*. The Shittah tree grew in the deserts of Sinai and the desert area around the Dead Sea. The wood is hard, heavy, and nearly indestructible by insects; the wood has a fine grain, and is brownish-orange in color. It grows abundantly in dry places and sometimes reaches a height of twenty feet and it yields lovely yellow flowers. Acacia wood was also used to make mummy-cases and fine furniture. This acacia wood undoubtedly foreshadows the humanity of Jesus Christ. Like this wood, we are told that his humanity would never see corruption: *"Men and brethren let me freely speak unto you of the patriarch David that he is both dead and buried, and his sepulcher is with us unto this day. Therefore being a prophet, and knowing that God had sworn with an oath to him, that of the fruit of his loins, according to the flesh, he would raise up Christ to sit on his throne; he seeing this before spake of the resurrection of Christ, that his soul was not left in hell, neither his flesh did see corruption"* (Acts 2:29–31). Peter here quotes King David, from Psalm 16:10: *"For you will not leave my soul in hell [Sheol], neither will thou suffer thine holy one to see corruption."*

Badger Skins:

Badger skins were the fourth and final outer covering for the tabernacle structure. This covering was visible for everyone to see. It was not just one large covering, but was made of many skins connected together. It was unattractive, coarse, and very plain in appearance. This speaks of how skeptical mankind viewed Jesus. There was no outward beauty to this tabernacle covering, and the same was said of Jesus Christ when he came to earth. Even the messianic prophet Isaiah prophesied seven hundred years before Jesus Christ came to earth saying: *"Who has believed our report? And to whom has the arm of the Lord been revealed? For he shall grow up before him as a tender plant, and as a root out of dry ground. He has no form or comeliness; and when we see him, there is no beauty that we should desire him" (Isaiah 53:1–2).* This is a picture of how Jesus appeared to many of that day; they viewed him as nothing more than a coarse, strange man, with a strange message. And, in far too many instances, people today still hold that view of Jesus Christ: nothing more than a coarse, strange man with a strange message.

But, to those whom the spirit leads to receive him, he is the altogether lovely one, the rose of Sharon, the lily of the valley, and the fairest among an enumerable number. Anyone who looks beyond the outer flesh covering will see Christ in all his glory. Remember Nathaniel's question: *"Can there any good thing come out of Nazareth?"* And Phillip says: *"Come and see" (John 1:46).* This disrespectful view of Jesus has been present from his early days on earth and scripture confirms it (see confirming scriptures below). *"He was in the world, and the world was made by him, and the world knew him not. He came unto his own, and his own received him not. But to as many as received him, to them gave he the power to become the sons of God, even to them that believe on his name: which were born, not of blood, nor of the will of the flesh, nor of the will of man, but of God. And the word was made flesh, and dwelt among us, and we beheld his glory the glory as of the only begotten of the father, full of grace and truth" (John 1:10–14).* Mankind, absent the baptism of the Holy Spirit, cannot see Jesus. But we see him … Selah!

Jesus Christ's Unceasing Presence

In The Linen Fence

When the building of the Tabernacle complex was finished, their first view, as mankind approached it, was the surrounding linen fence. The instructions for the tabernacle are very detailed and treatment of the linen fence is no different. God gave precise instructions to his servant Moses in Exodus: *"And thou shalt make the court of the tabernacle: for the south side, southward there shall be hangings for the court of fine twined linen of an hundred cubits long for one side: And the twenty pillars thereof and their twenty sockets shall be of brass; the hooks of the pillars and their fillets shall be of silver. And likewise for the north side in length there shall be hangings of an hundred cubits long, and his twenty pillars and their twenty sockets of brass; the hooks of the pillars and their fillets of silver. And for the breadth of the court on the west side shall be hangings of fifty cubits: their pillars ten, and their sockets ten. And the breadth of the court on the east side eastward shall be fifty cubits. The hangings of one side of the gate shall be fifteen cubits: their pillars three, and their sockets three. And on the other side shall be hangings fifteen cubits: their pillars three, and their sockets three. And for the gate of the court shall be an hanging of twenty cubits, of blue, and purple, and scarlet, and fine twined linen, wrought with needlework: and their pillars shall be four, and their sockets four. All the pillars round about the court shall be filleted with silver; their hooks shall be of silver, and their sockets of brass. The length of the court shall be an hundred cubits, and the breadth fifty, and the height five cubits of fine twined linen, and their sockets of brass. All the vessels of the tabernacle in all the service thereof, and all the pins thereof, and all the pins of the court, shall be of brass"* (Exodus 27:9–19).

The entire tabernacle structure was enclosed by this massive, curtain fence, which was five cubit, or seven and a half feet high. The outer court around the structure was 150 feet long on the north and south sides and 75 feet long on the west side, but only 45 feet long on the east side, leaving room for the entrance gate. For ease of assembly, the fence was divided into five manageable lengths, as opposed to one overwhelmingly long curtain. These five separate curtains formed the barrier around the courtyard. Two of these curtains ran along the north and south sides. One ran along the west end, while two short curtains ran on either side of the front entrance gate. The plain white linen screen fence formed a protection around the tabernacle, the dwelling place of God on earth. No Israelite could casually wander around the holy building, or casually stroll into the courtyard. Fine white linen material symbolizes righteousness, as when the bride of Christ makes herself ready for the wedding. Her wedding dress was to be made of fine linen to symbolize righteousness: *"And to her was granted that she should be arrayed in fine linen, clean and white: for the fine linen is the righteousness of saints" (Revelation 19:8).* The wall of fine linen around the tabernacle barred anyone whose thoughts or actions would not be righteous before God, preventing access to the courtyard except through the proper entrance gate, sometimes referred to as the door.

The fence was stabilized with pins and cords mentioned in Exodus 35:18. The bronze pins were like large nails or spikes. They were driven into the ground, and the cords were attached to them to give the tabernacle tent strength and protection from wind and the elements. The scriptures discuss pins, stakes, and cords in other places. For example, Isaiah 22:23 states: *"And I will fasten him as a nail in a sure place; and he shall be for a glorious throne to his father's house."* Also, Isaiah 54:2 reads: *"Enlarge the place of thy tent, and let them stretch forth the curtains of thine habitations: spare not, lengthen thy cords, and strengthen thy stakes."*

The Spiritual Essence of the Linen Fence

The fine white linen fence represents the righteousness of God's total perfection. Jesus Christ is also the righteousness of God to those who embrace his work at the cross. We also read at 2 Corinthians 5:21 *that believers have been made the righteousness of God.* So, believers no longer have a righteousness of their own. God describes all of what unregenerate mankind calls righteousness as filthy rags. Jesus Christ, in his dying for humanity, bore our sin and shed his blood to pay the sin-debt, for all mankind. Thus he is called the end of the law because the righteousness of Christ has fulfilled the old law for all who will receive him. Therefore, when God sees believers conducting their affairs on earth righteously, he sees the righteousness of Jesus Christ. The question has been asked: how good must one be to enter heaven? The answer is: "as perfect as Christ himself." And he was without sin! Remember when the Jewish leaders wanted to stone him, he asked: *"For which good work will you stone me?"(John 10:32).*

If a man without Christ were to lift the mercy seat and gaze into the Ark of the Covenant, he would come face-to-face with the *law of God.* Without the covering of the shed blood of Jesus, he would face instant death. The believer must live so as to say: *"I am crucified with Christ: nevertheless I live; yet not I but Christ liveth in me; and the life which I now live in the flesh I live by the faith of the Son of God, who loved me and gave himself for me"* (Galatians 2:20). And all believers must stand in the earth as the wall of righteousness, guarding and protecting the holiness of God.

THE ENTRANCE GATE

We learned earlier that when an Israelite citizen approached the tabernacle, the dwelling place of God, they found an outer wall of white linen, which formed a barricade against their entrance. However, there was one stretch of fence twenty cubits, or 30 feet wide, which was different and always accessible. It was known as the entrance gate, sometimes called the door. The linen of this gate was *multicolored, woven of white, blue, purple, and scarlet.* The curtains for this gate section hung on four strong pillars. This entrance is clearly identified as the one way through which the person in need of atonement could gain access to the courts of almighty God. The gate, with its blend of white, blue, purple, and scarlet, is described in Exodus 27:16. *"And for the gate of the court shall be an hanging of twenty cubits, of blue, and purple, and scarlet, and fine twined linen, wrought with needlework: and their pillars shall be four, and their sockets four."* This gate was identical to the gate, or door-hanging, at the entrance to the tabernacle structure in this complex. This gate that is the only way into the tabernacle complex, reminds us of a familiar passage of scripture in John 14:6 where Jesus says: *"No man cometh to the father but by me."* The gate was noticeably different from the white linen fence and was the single way into the entire tabernacle complex: the one and only entrance through which men and women could draw near to God. Whether a priests who had duties in the tabernacle, or just a repentant sinner seeking forgiveness for his misdeeds, all had to enter by that one way.

Any Israelite approaching the tabernacle leading his sacrifice behind him and desiring atonement knew that there was only one way to reach the bronze/brazen altar; they also knew that way was through this eastward gate which was always open, always available for access. It was never barred; there was nothing to forbid the pursuit of the presence of God. However, it was true then, and is true today; one must make a personal decision to enter by this gate. Today if one is to regain the glory and presence of mankind's original status and relationship with God, they must enter through the door who is Jesus; he is the only way to the father.

Students of this class often asked why the tabernacle faced east. The simple answer is, God's instructions required an eastern orientation *(see Numbers 2:3; 3:38, Ezekiel 43:1, and Matthew 24:27).*

While those with clean motives were welcome, it was always clear there would be no foolishness. Notice, "On the east side, toward the rising of the sun, where the entrance gate is located, Israel's *"standard of the forces"* [Israel's armed forces] were arrayed with the camp of Judah nearest to the tabernacle; and after that each tribe camped according to the size of their army." (To study the arrangement of the camp of Israel around the tabernacle in the wilderness, see *Numbers 2:1–34).*

Spiritual Essence of the Gate/Door

The gate located on the east side of the tabernacle, the only available access to God for lost humanity, points to salvation, through the flesh and blood of Jesus Christ. He became our door, our entrance, our gate, our pathway to God of the scriptures. This is the gate to the court so often referred to in God's Word: *"We will enter his gates with Thanksgiving in our hearts; we will enter his courts with praise." (Read Psalms 84:2, 10; and 100:4–5.)*

To assure that current-day humanity fully appreciates the importance of Jesus as the door, we look historically at the importance of the gate/door.

Jesus is able to stand as the gate/door for the whole world, because he has a history: he is the second person of the Godhead; he is one with the Father and the Holy Spirit; and in no way new to the Bible scene. We learned earlier that the prophet Isaiah saw him in a vision seven hundred years before he came to earth. And John, the writer of Revelation, experienced him in a vision: *"And one of the elders saith unto me, weep not: behold, the lion of the tribe of Judah, the root of David, hath prevailed to open the book, and to loose the seven seals thereof. And I beheld, and, lo, in the midst of the throne and of the four beasts, and in the midst of the elders, stood a lamb as it had been slain, having seven horns and seven eyes, which are the seven spirits of God sent forth into all the earth. And he came and took the book out of the right hand of him that sat upon the throne. And when he had taken the book, the four beasts and four and twenty elders fell down before the lamb, having every one of them harps, and golden vials full of odors, which are the prayers of saints. And they sung a new song, saying, Thou art worthy to take the book, and to open the seals thereof: for thou wast slain, and hast redeemed us to God by thy blood out of every kindred, and tongue, and people, and nation; And hast made us unto our God kings and priests: and we shall reign on the earth"* (Revelation 5:5–10). Further, in Revelation 5:11–14 we read: *"Then I looked, and I heard the voice of many angels around the throne, the living creatures, and the elders; and the number of them was ten thousand times ten thousand, and thousands of thousands, saying with a loud voice worthy is the Lamb who was slain to receive power and riches and wisdom, and strength and honor and glory and blessing!" And every creature which is in heaven and on the earth and under the earth and such as are in the sea, and all that are in them I heard saying: "Blessing and honor and glory and power be to him who sits on the throne, and to the lamb, forever and ever!" Then the four living creatures said, "Amen!" And the twenty-four elders fell down and worshiped him who lives forever and ever."*

In the present-day spiritual universe, where God, Jesus, and true believers live, we must never lose sight of the fact that he is Lord over every earthly lord, and King over every earthly king; he is our access to the believer's inheritance.

In the old tabernacle, the priest who came to the tabernacle for daily ministry first approached the altar, atoned for himself, before he approached ***the entrance door*** of the holy place to perform effective ministry. In the new covenant likewise, the believer/priest must first be redeemed by the blood of Jesus at the altar of the *cross of Christ*, be cleansed, and consecrated through fervent prayer to receive the anointing for effective ministry, before he is allowed into the presence of God. The whole world must know that Jesus Christ is the door to God's throne; he is always accessible to all mankind, believers and non-believers alike. All humanity is invited to come through him and find enduring peace in true relationship with God of the scriptures.

The Word of God says about those who embrace him, *"We are able to therefore come boldly to the throne of grace that we may obtain mercy and find grace to help in our time of need" (Hebrews. 4:16).* Also, we read in John: *"Then said Jesus unto them again, verily, verily, I say unto you, I am the door of the sheep. All that ever came before me are thieves and robbers: but the sheep did not hear them. I am the door: by me if any man enters in, he shall be saved, and shall go in and out, and find pasture" (John 10:7–9).*

World leaders who seek peace are unwittingly in search of the prince of peace. Many in the church are also in search of the peace of Jesus Christ; one who finds Jesus finds peace. *"Peace I leave with you, my peace I give unto you: not as the world giveth, give I unto you. Let not your heart be troubled, neither let it be afraid" (John 14:27).*

For some believers, Messiah is yet to come, and for others he is coming back. Nevertheless, many in the church are looking for peace.

Peace is not a thing, a state of mind, a formula, or agreement among mankind. Peace comes from knowing the prince of peace; his name is Jesus. Peter said it this way: *"Grace and peace be multiplied unto you through the knowledge of God, and of Jesus our Lord, according as his divine power hath given unto us all things that pertain unto life and godliness, through the knowledge of him that hath called us to glory and virtue: Whereby are given unto us exceeding great and precious promises: that by these ye might be partakers of the divine nature, having escaped the corruption that is in the world through lust. And beside this, giving all diligence, add to your faith virtue; and to virtue knowledge; and to knowledge temperance; and to temperance patience; and to patience godliness; and to godliness brotherly kindness; and to brotherly kindness charity. For if these things be in you, and abound, they make you that ye shall neither be barren nor unfruitful in the knowledge of our Lord Jesus Christ. But he that lacketh these things is blind, and cannot see afar off, and hath forgotten that he was purged from his old sins. Wherefore the rather, brethren, give diligence to make your calling and election sure: for if ye do these things, ye shall never fall: For so an entrance shall be ministered unto you abundantly into the everlasting kingdom of our Lord and Savior Jesus Christ"* (2 Peter 1:2–11).

Yes, there is much symbolism in this Old Testament Tabernacle; research the scriptures for its meaning, it is highly instructive and enormously useful to the comprehension of salvation revealed in both the Old and New Testament scriptures, especially for current-day saints and their churches.

THE OUTER COURT

We have now entered through the entrance gate and into the outer court, (the yard around the tabernacle building). It is helpful to remember that Moses built this tabernacle when the nation of Israel was on the move through the Sinai wilderness on their march from bondage in Egypt, to the Promised Land. This entire tabernacle complex was portable. The two-section tabernacle building was a structure of wooden framework covered with gold. The first section was called the sanctuary, or the Holy Place. The second section was the Holy of Holies; it was God's actual dwelling place on earth and was a foreshadowing replica of God's true and authentic throne room in heaven. The tabernacle building stood in the western half of this rectangular outer courtyard and its entrance faced east. When the tabernacle construction was completed in accordance with the instructions God gave to Moses on the mount, the presence of God's spirit, the shekinah glory of God, manifested itself as a cloud and descended upon the tabernacle, confirming God's approval and acceptance. When the work was finished in accordance with God's instructions, the scriptures say: *"And Moses was not able to enter into the tent of the congregation, because the cloud abode thereon, and the glory of the Lord filled the tabernacle. And when the cloud was taken up from over the tabernacle, the children of Israel went onward in all their journeys: But if the cloud were not taken up, then they journeyed not till the day that it was taken up. For the cloud of the Lord was upon the tabernacle by day, and fire was upon it by night, in the sight of all the house of Israel, throughout all their journeys" (Exodus 40:34–38).*

These passages teach us several important things. For one, God gave his approval of the finished work of the tabernacle by sending his presence as a *cloud by day* and a *fire by night.* Also, God was providing for the needs of the nation of Israel in this desert location; they would have needed the shade of the cloud during the heat of the day, and warmth of the pillar of fire in the coolness of the nights. Also, we learn that God was providing visible guidance for Israel through the cloud. When the *Cloud of God* moved to a different location, the Israelites moved the tabernacle to wherever the cloud settled. While it is true God doesn't change, he does move. So the people of God, and particularly his church, must always be vigilant to discern the movement of God's spirit, and be watchful not to get stuck in a place where God once was. *Selah.*

Any Israelite citizen could enter this outer court. However, only the priests, Aaron and his sons, could go beyond the first veil, the first compartment of the tabernacle structure. *Note:* There were many **sons of Levi** who ministered in the tabernacle who were not called priests, but were members of the Levitical camp. There were so many Levites that they were assigned to three groups, the **Kohath** group with 8,600 members, the **Gershon** group with 7,500 members, and the **Merari** group with 6,200. All these groups were Levites; however, only Aaron, his sons, and Moses were Priests who could enter the tabernacle's holy spaces. The high priest, Aaron, was allowed to bring a sacrifice for the sins of the people beyond the second veil into the Holy of Holies into the presence of God once a year. The sacrificial offering of animal blood that he made was for temporary atonement, and needed repeating annually. That "*blood of a substitute system*" for sinful mankind was a foreshadowing of an acceptable approach into God's presence: the way in which the ultimate High Priest Jesus Christ would present his own sacrificed blood to pay mankind's sin-debt and gain our perpetual redemption.

The Word of God to Moses was very specific regarding how the Israelites were to approach God. The nation had never physically approached God while in the slave camps of Egypt. God had offered to reveal himself to the people at Mount Sinai, but they were horrified at that idea and decided that no man except Moses should approach God (see *Exodus 19:7–25; 20:18–23*). God desired that all Israel become a "*kingdom of priests*". He also desires that his current-day church become a kingdom of priests: *"But, ye are a chosen generation, a royal priesthood, an holy nation, a peculiar people; that ye should show forth the praises of him who hath called you out of darkness into his marvelous light and come boldly to the throne of Grace" (1 Peter 2:9).*

There, in the Sinai wilderness, through the tabernacle and the Israeli nation, God demonstrated to all mankind, an acceptable pattern for sinful man to approach his (God's) presence. It was there, with the demonstration of this substitutionary pattern that God began to reveal what was involved in the arrangement of *the substitutionary shedding of blood* as an acceptable sacrifice for sin. Thus, it was there, in the tabernacle, that the method for the substitutionary sacrifice to redeem all mankind by Jesus Christ was established. Hallelujah!

This Old Testament system of atonement was initiated when an Israeli citizen became personally aware that they had transgressed God's commandments and recognized that sin had contaminated their life and separated them from God (*Isaiah 59:1–5*). With personal acceptance of their need for God's forgiveness, they made their way to the God-appointed place of atonement. Starting in the outer court of the tabernacle, they steered their sin-sacrifice through the process until its blood, along with the blood of many other sacrifices, was presented by the high priest before God in the Holy of Holies. Today, we must come to the supernatural throne-room of God and, by faith, spiritually accept the sacrificial work of Jesus Christ, our lamb, who shed his own blood and poured it on the altar of heaven to atone for our sins.

Here in the outer court as we move in the direction of the presence of God, we would come next to the brazen altar of sacrifice.

THE BRAZEN/BRONZE ALTAR:

Now we take an in-depth look at the brazen altar. Upon entering the outer court, the brazen altar is the first piece of furniture we encounter, often referred to as the bronze altar, or the burning altar. *"And thou shalt make an altar of shittim wood, five cubits long, and five cubits broad; the altar shall be foursquare: and the height thereof shall be three cubits. And thou shalt make the horns of it upon the four corners thereof: his horns shall be of the same: and thou shalt overlay it with brass. And thou shalt make his pans to receive his ashes, and his shovels, and his basons, and his fleshhooks, and firepans: all the vessels thereof thou shalt make of brass. And thou shalt make for it a grate a network of brass; and upon the net shalt thou make four brasen rings in the four corners thereof. And thou shalt put it under the compass of the altar beneath that the net may be even to the midst of the altar. And thou shalt make staves for the altar, staves of shittim wood, and overlay them with brass. And the staves shall be put into the rings, and the staves shall be upon the two sides of the altar, to bear it. Hollow with boards shalt thou make it: as it was shewed thee in the mount, so shall they make it"* (Exodus 27:1–8).

When an Israelite approached the tabernacle with their sacrifice as they passed through the entrance gate into the outer court, they found that between them and the tabernacle structure where God dwelled was the brazen altar with priests waiting beside it. The altar was square in shape. Its height was three cubits, or 4 1/2 feet, and it was made of acacia/shittim wood. It was overlaid with bronze with horns at each of its four corners.

At this altar, the priest guided the process of the sacrificial offering of the person seeking atonement. Though the offering-seeker was personally required to kill or to sacrifice the animal, the priest ministered oversight. This altar was where the sacrificial blood of bulls and calves and goats was shed and sinners were pardoned. God specified the offerings to be brought: *"And the Lord called unto Moses, and spake unto him out of the tabernacle of the congregation, saying, speak unto the children of Israel, and say unto them, if any man of you brings an offering unto the Lord, ye shall bring your offering of the cattle, even of the herd, and of the flock. If his offering be a burnt sacrifice of the herd, let him offer a male without blemish: he shall offer it of his own voluntary will at the door of the tabernacle of the congregation before the Lord. And he shall put his hand upon the head of the burnt offering; and it shall be accepted for him to make atonement for him. And he shall kill the bullock before the Lord: and the priests, Aaron's sons, shall bring the blood, and sprinkle the blood round about upon the altar that is by the door of the tabernacle of the congregation. And he shall flay the burnt offering, and cut it into his pieces. And the sons of Aaron the priest shall put fire upon the altar, and lay the wood in order upon the fire: And the priests, Aaron's sons, shall lay the parts, the head, and the fat, in order upon the wood that is on the fire which is upon the altar: But inwards and legs shall he wash in water: and the priest shall burn all on the altar, to be a burnt sacrifice, an offering made by fire, of a sweet savour unto the Lord"* (Leviticus 1:1–9).

No matter how kind hearted or helpful or pleasant a person is, without the shedding of blood there is no forgiveness or remission for sin. God is not a man and he cannot lie. He said: *"For the life of the flesh is in the blood: and I have given it to you upon the altar to make atonement for your souls [really this word is spirit]: for it is the blood that maketh atonement for the soul" (Leviticus 17:11).*

Without the brazen/bronze altar, there was no acceptable approach to God. Covenants made with God were blood covenants, and it was at this altar that innocent animals stood in the sinner's stead. Here the sinner was required to lay hands upon the innocent animal-sacrifice and violently slit its throat. This graphic imagery was intended to bring an incredible awareness of the awesome ugliness of sin and to provide an enhanced awareness that the payment for sin is death. Only with such awareness, understanding, and acceptance of this truth could the sinner reach the state of mind required to be declared clean. Keep in mind, that the blood of an animal-sacrifice in the stead of sinful man was a temporary measure until God himself in the person of Jesus Christ, the Lamb of God, would come to take away sin once and for all. Here, the priest would catch the animal's blood in a basin and pour the blood out at the foot of the altar, thus making the sacrifice complete. When this process was finished the sinner walked away forgiven until their next sin. The priests administered these sacrifices throughout the year, but the yearly sacrifice was made on behalf of the entire nation of Israel by the high priest himself on the Day of Atonement.

In the Hebrew language the word altar means, "Place where sacrifice is made". An altar is also a place where that which is sacrificed is lifted up. The sacrifice was lifted up and lowered as the priests would raise or lower the grating of the bronze/burning altar. This altar remained continuously lifted up above the ground as it was built to assure that the grating upon which the sacrifice laid was always three feet above the ground. It connotes a sacrifice being lifted up before the Lord, as if it were physically being lifted to the Lord. It reminds us of the familiar words in John 12:32: *"And I, if I be lifted up from the earth, I will draw all men unto me."* It was customary during Old Testament times for those who wished to please God to build an altar, often made of stone, and there they called upon the name of the Lord. (For examples, see *Genesis 8:20; 12:7–8; 26:25; 33:20; and 35:2–3.)*

This brazen altar of sacrifice was the largest of the tabernacle vessels, signifying the importance of sacrifice. Without sacrifice for atonement, humankind's approach to God would come to a screeching halt. This altar was larger than all the other furniture or instruments combined. It was made of acacia wood connoting indestructibility. It was overlaid with bronze to withstand heat (bronze also indicates judgment *Numbers 21:8–9 and John 3:14–16).* This entire altar was made of materials from the earth created by God. It contained nothing made or manufactured by man. Exodus 20:25–26 says: *"And if thou wilt make me an altar of stone, thou shalt not build it of hewn stone: for if thou lift up thy tool upon it, thou hast polluted it. Neither shalt thou go up by steps unto mine altar, that thy nakedness be not discovered thereon."*

The horns of the altar are described in Exodus 27:2: *"You shall make its horns on its four corners; its horns shall be of one piece with it. And you shall overlay it with bronze."* The altar's four horns signify God's unlimited universal power. Horns symbolize the strength of an animal, or the power of a person, or nation. See Psalm 89:17: *"For you are the glory of their strength, and in your favor our horn is exalted."* There's no limit to God's power and he uses it on behalf of those who sacrifice before him.

"You shall take some of the blood of the bull and put it on the horns of the altar with your finger, and pour all the blood beside the base of the altar" (Exodus 29:12). There was power in the blood of the substitute-sacrificial animals to bring temporary atonement; as it was sprinkled on the horns of the altar, there was a connection between the altar, the horns, and the sinner.

The four horns on the altar's corners were also used to leash an animal waiting to be sacrificed. As mentioned earlier, the horns of the altar were also seen as a place of refuge. A man accused of murder could grab hold of one of these horns for safety. If he was innocent, the horn would protect him. *"He that smiteth a man, so that he dies shall be surely put to death. And if a man lie not in wait but God deliver him into his hand; then I will appoint thee a place whither he shall flee. But if a man come presumptuously upon his neighbor, to slay him with guile; thou shalt take him from mine altar, that he may die"* (Exodus, 21:12–14).

The Bible gives us the story of Adonijah. Fearing the rule of the new King Solomon, his elder brother Adonijah went and took hold of the altar's horns for safety: *"And Adonijah feared because of Solomon; and arose, and went and caught hold of the horns of the altar"* (1 Kings 1:50). There is another example that involves Joab who was King David's lifelong military commander (see 1 Kings 2:28–33).

As mentioned earlier, the sacrifices were also leashed with cords to the horns. *"God is the Lord, which hath shewed us light: bind the sacrifice with cords, even unto the horns of the altar"* (Psalm 118:27).

THE UTENSILS OF THE BRAZEN/BRONZE ALTAR:

"And thou shalt make his (it's) pans to receive his ashes, and his shovels, and his basins, and his fleshhooks, and his firepans: all the vessels thereof thou shalt make of brass. And thou shalt make for it a grate of network of brass; and upon the net shalt thou make four brazen rings in the four corners thereof" (Exodus 27:3–4).

The Pans

The Pans were used to receive the ashes from the burnt sacrifice. Great care was given to these ashes; they were disposed of outside the camp, but in a clean place. They were precious because they spoke of the finality of God's acceptance of the offered sacrifice. And they were often used during times of grief and mourning, or when people needed forgiveness. It was a custom in such times to sit in ashes or pour them on their heads; or they would clothe themselves in sackcloth and ashes and pray. Ashes are also a symbol of the complete destruction of a thing, symbolizing that the ordeal with their transgression was finalized. *"And whosoever toucheth one that is slain with a sword in the open fields, or a dead body, or a bone of a man, or a grave, shall be unclean seven days.*

And for an unclean person they shall take of the ashes of the burnt heifer of purification for sin, and running water shall be put thereto in a vessel: And a clean person shall take hyssop, and dip it in the water, and sprinkle it upon the tent, and upon all the vessels, and upon the persons that were there, and upon him that touched a bone, of one slain, or one dead, or a grave: And the clean person shall sprinkle upon the unclean on the third day, and on the seventh day: and on the seventh day he shall purify himself, and wash his clothes, and bathe himself in water, and shall be clean at even" (Numbers 19:16–19).

The Shovels

These shovels were used to clear away the ashes from the altar.

The Basins

The basins were used by the priest to catch the blood of the sacrificed animal. The blood would then be sprinkled and poured out at the bottom of the altar.

Fire Pans

These pans were the censers used to carry the fire (burning coals) from the brazen altar of burnt offerings for service at the altar of incense. The brazen altar of burnt offerings supplied the fire used at the altar of incense (see *Leviticus 16:11–14*). There is a decidedly edifying and useful historical record regarding these brazen/bronze altar instruments found in the book of Isaiah. *"In the year that King Uzziah died I saw also the Lord sitting upon a throne, high and lifted up, and his train filled the temple. Above it stood the seraphim: each one had six wings; with twain (two) he covered his face, and with twain he covered his feet, and with twain he did fly. And one cried unto another, and said, holy, holy, holy, is the Lord of hosts: the whole earth is full of his glory. And the posts of the door moved at the voice of him that cried, and the house was filled with smoke. Then said I, woe is me! For I am undone; because I am a man of unclean lips, and I dwell in the midst of a people of unclean lips: for mine eyes have seen the King, the Lord of hosts. Then flew one of the seraphim unto me, having a live coal in his hand, which he had taken with the tongs from off the altar: and he laid it upon my mouth, and said, lo, this hath touched thy lips; and thine iniquity is taken away, and thy sin purged. Also I heard the voice of the Lord, saying, whom shall I send, and who will go for us? Then said I, here am I; send me." (Isaiah 6:1–8).* Until the cleansing, purging coals of the altar touched and purified Isaiah's lips, he recognized that he was an unfit vessel in the face of God whose train filled the temple, but once he was cleansed he was qualified to offer himself in the service of a holy God. As a clean and holy vessel he was qualified to say, *'here am I; send me'*.

The Bronze Grating

This altar contained a grating also made of bronze that rested on a ledge inside the brazen altar where the slain animals were placed. This grating could be raised or lowered as needed and it would allow the fat to drip down and fall below. When sacrificing occurred, the grating was the same height from the ground as the *mercy seat,* indicating balanced equality between decisions of mercy and judgment: *"Behold therefore the goodness and severity of God: On them which fell [suffered] severity; but toward thee [saints] goodness, if thou continue in his goodness: otherwise thou also shalt be cut off. And they also, if they abide not still in unbelief, shall be grafted in: for God is able to graft them in again"* (Romans 11:22–23). The scripture simply says God is fair; judgment will be upon all who fall away, but grace if they correct their ways. Likewise, grace will be upon those who continue to obey; however, if they fall away, they also will be cut off.

The Fire

The fire on the altar was originally ignited by God himself and was never to be extinguished: *"And there came a fire out from before the Lord, and consumed upon the altar the burnt offering and the fat: which when all the people saw, they shouted, and fell on their faces" (Leviticus 9:24).* Also see: *"And the fire upon the altar shall be burning in it; it shall not be put out: and the priest shall burn wood on it every morning, and lay the burnt offering in order upon it; and he shall burn thereon the fat of the peace offerings. The fire shall ever be burning upon the altar; it shall never go out" (Leviticus. 6:12–13).* Fire was symbolic of the presence of the Holy Spirit and his power that was used for approval or for destruction: *"And it came to pass, that in the morning watch the Lord looked unto the host of the Egyptians through the pillar of fire and of the cloud, and troubled the host of the Egyptians" (Exodus 14:24).* We learned earlier that the pillars of fire came to show God's approval at the completion of the tabernacle; but he used the fire also to show his displeasure. *"And when the people complained, it displeased the Lord: and the Lord heard it; and his anger was kindled; and the fire of the Lord burnt among them, and consumed them that were in the uttermost parts of the camp" (Numbers 11:1).* Here the Lord used this power for destruction. Also, the Lord appeared in the burning bush on Mount Horeb, and out of the burning bush he called one of his greatest leaders, Moses, who led all of Israel. *"Now Moses kept the flock of Jethro his father in law, the priest of Midian: and he led the flock to the backside of the desert, and came to the mountain of God, even to Horeb. And the angel of the Lord appeared unto him in a flame of fire out of the midst of a bush: and he looked, and, beholds, the bush burned with fire, and the bush was not consumed. And Moses said, I will now turn aside, and see this great sight, why the bush is not burnt. And when the Lord saw that he turned aside to see, God called unto him out of the midst of the bush, and said, Moses, Moses. And he said here am I, and he said, draw not nigh hither: put off thy shoes from off thy feet, for the place whereon thou standest is holy ground" (Exodus 3:1–5)*. The Lord showed himself in the midst of fire to Isaiah, Ezekiel, and John the Revelator.

Spiritual Essence of the Brazen/Bronze Altar

Through God's unfolding revelation, it is now clear that the sins of all those who believed God in the old tabernacle sacrificial system were later recompensed by the blood of Christ. Though the sin-debt of these earlier sinners could not be fully paid by the periodic animal sacrifices, for they could only bring short-term forgiveness, perpetuity would take the cleansing blood of Jesus Christ, the Lamb of God, slain before the foundation of the world, to permanently erase their sin-debt. You see, the blood of Jesus cleanses not just the body, but also the conscience of all mankind. The book of Hebrews makes this very clear. *"Then verily the first covenant had also ordinances of divine service, and a worldly sanctuary. For there was a tabernacle made; the first, wherein was the candlestick, and the table, and the shewbread; which is called the sanctuary. And after the second veil, the tabernacle which is called the Holiest of all; Which had the golden censer, and the ark of the covenant overlaid roundabout with gold, wherein was the golden pot that had manna, and Aaron's rod that budded, and the tables of the covenant; And over it the cherubim of glory shadowing the mercy seat; of which we cannot now speak particularly. Now when these things were thus ordained, the priests went always into the first tabernacle, accomplishing the services of God. But into the second went the high priest alone once every year, not without blood, which he offered for himself, and for the errors of the people: The holy ghost thus signifying, that the way into the holiest of all was not yet made manifest, while as the first tabernacle was yet standing: which was a figure for the time then present, in which were offered both gifts and sacrifices, that could not make him that did the service perfect, as pertaining to the conscience; which stood only in meats and drinks, and divers washings, and carnal ordinances, imposed on them until the time of reformation. But Christ being come an high priest of good things to come, by a greater and more perfect tabernacle, not made with hands, that is to say, not of this building; Neither by the blood of goats and calves, but by his own blood he entered in once into the holy place, having obtained eternal redemption for us [all]. For if the blood of bulls and of goats, and the ashes of a heifer sprinkling the unclean, sanctifieth to the purifying of the flesh: How much more shall the blood of Christ, who through the eternal spirit offered himself without spot to God, purge your conscience from dead works to serve the living God? (Hebrews 9:1–14).*

Without the fullness of the power of the Spirit of God *[the baptism of the Holy Spirit]* living inside believers, the flesh will always play a major role in the believer's life, worship, and their church. Christ died to change that. And for believers to continue to live life without the full power of the baptism, full faith in the work of the Holy Spirit, is to live beneath the believer's privileges.

THE BRONZE LAVER

As you may have noticed, God was meticulous in his instructions regarding the making of the Tabernacle, its furnishings, and utensils. Let's review the instructions he gave to Moses to make the bronze laver and proceed from that understanding. *"And the Lord spake unto Moses, saying, Thou shalt also make a laver of brass, and his [its] foot also of brass, to wash withal: and thou shalt put it between the tabernacle of the congregation and the altar, and thou shalt put water therein. For Aaron and his sons shall wash their hands and their feet thereat: when they go into the tabernacle of the congregation, they shall wash with water, that they die not; or when they come near to the altar to minister, to burn offering made by fire unto the Lord: so they shall wash their hands and their feet, that they die not: and it shall be a statute forever to them, even to him and to his seed throughout their generations"* (Exodus 30:17–21).

It was here at the bronze laver that the priests washed their hands and feet before entering and leaving the holy place. This bronze laver was strategically located between the two major places where the priests spent their time in ministry: the holy place called the sanctuary, and at the brazen burning altar, located in the outer court. Absolutely no ministry was acceptable to the Lord without cleansing. So serious was any violation of this divine order, that to ignore it meant death. Look again at Exodus

30:20–21 above. No ministry that excluded a visit to the brazen laver of cleansing is ever acceptable to God. Imagine the degree of spiritual death that comes into the church today because both priests and believers fail to visit the laver of cleansing through confession, repentance, and fervent prayer for forgiveness before entering into sanctuary worship.

The material to make the laver came from melting the bronze mirrors brought out of Egypt by the Israelite women. It was filled with water for the continual cleansing of the priests as they ministered in the work of the Lord. *"And he made the laver of brass, and the foot of it of brass from the looking glasses of the women, which assembled at the door of the tabernacle of the congregation"* (Exodus 38:8).

The Mirrors of the Wives

During that time in history, mirrors were made of highly polished bronze. It is widely accepted by theologians that bronze represents judgment. The bronze mirrors used to make the laver were two-sided disks with a concave side that had a thick raised rim and a convex side that was highly polished decorated bronze. The laver was made from solid bronze mirrors; no wood or other material was used. *"And he made the laver of brass, and the foot of it of brass, of the looking glasses of the women assembling, which assembled at the door of the tabernacle of the congregation"* (Exodus 38:8). The bronze typifies the judgment Christ accepted when he stood beneath the sins of the whole world and took upon himself the fire of God's judgment and justice. In all of this, God's plan was at work, although humanity did not fully understand it at the time. When the Hebrew people were in Egypt, though they were slaves, they departed Egypt with most of the materials needed to construct God's tabernacle in the wilderness. *"But every woman shall borrow of her neighbour and of her that sojourneth in her house, jewels of silver, and jewels of gold, and raiment: and ye shall put them upon your sons, and upon your daughters; and ye shall spoil the Egyptians"* (Exodus 3:22).

It is said that a total of 6,700 pounds of bronze came out of Egypt and was strategically used in all the places where exceptional heat resisting materials were needed. Bronze has a melting point of 1,985 degrees. It was important in the brazen altar, where intense heat was continually present. Notice that God not only instructed the women to borrow from their neighbor, but he gave the same instruction to the men: *"Speak now in the ears of the people, and let every man borrow of his neighbour, and every woman of her neighbour, jewels of silver and jewels of gold" (Exodus 11:2).* In Exodus 12 we read: *"And the children of Israel did according to the word of Moses; and they borrowed of the Egyptians jewels of silver, and jewels of gold, and raiment: And the Lord gave the people favour in the sight of the Egyptians, so that they lent (gave) unto them such things as they required and they spoiled the Egyptians" (Exodus 12:35–36).* Here we see an example of the rewards for obedience to the Word of God, whether the word proceeds directly from the mouth of God or through his established leader.

The Laver's Placement

On the path toward the Holy of Holies where God dwelt, the brazen laver came after the altar of burnt sacrifice. However, it came before the Holy Place. This order of arrangement was necessary because no unclean thing or person can approach near to God and live. As the priest entered the gate of the outer court, he also faced the brazen burning altar of sacrifice, where he made a sacrifice for himself, like any other Israelite. However, once he was beyond the burning altar, although he was a priest, it was only after he had cleansed himself at the laver that he was prepared for the service of God.

Once he was cleansed, his ministry was acceptable, either at the burning altar or in the Holy Place. The altar of sacrifice came first for the priest, then cleansing at the laver, and then service. The location of the laver was before one reached the door of the Holy Place because cleansing by the blood and the water must always happen before entering

God's presence, even to serve. Read the words of Jesus in this regard: *"Jesus answered, verily, verily, I say unto thee, except a man be born of water and of the spirit, he cannot enter into the kingdom of God" (John 3:5)*. Many read this scripture and think that *entering into the kingdom of God* happens only following physical death. No, the current day faith filled believer moves, by faith, between *this present corrupt world* and the *kingdom of God,* as often as they are led to do so by the spirit of God.

Everything beyond the door of the tabernacle's Holy Place were vessels that represented God himself. No priest dared enter this atmosphere with any trace of uncleanness for fear of death. *"Be holy as I am holy"* was then and still is commanded of the priests.

We learned that in the outer court, the furnishings were covered with solid bronze, signifying judgment. However, inside the Holy Place all things were covered with gold. Gold represents deity; throughout the scriptures pure gold speaks of divinity, which cannot be produced by man. This also means that gold represents the divine glory of our Lord Jesus Christ, who is God, who came to earth as God (The Christ) and man (Jesus of Nazareth), in the person called Jesus Christ: Isaiah 9:6 *"For unto us a child is born, unto us a son is given: and the government shall be upon his shoulder: and his name shall be called Wonderful, Counselor, The mighty God, The everlasting Father, The Prince of Peace".*

There are no measurements or instructions given for the shape and size of the laver. The only mention is that it had a stand, which made it easier for people to wash (see Exodus 31:9). There is a mystery as to just how the Israelis moved the laver when God's spirit cloud relocated because there is no mention of staves. The altar and other vessels had staves and rings that allowed them to be carried.

Moses at the Laver

It was at this laver that Moses himself washed the entire body of Aaron and his sons at their sanctification ceremony. In the following scripture, the word "wash" means to wash all over. Their bodies were washed first, and then their clothing. *"And thou shalt anoint the laver and his foot, and sanctify it. And thou shalt bring Aaron and his sons unto the door of the tabernacle of the congregation, and wash them with water. And thou shalt put upon Aaron the holy garments, and anoint him, and sanctify him; that he may minister unto me in the priest's office. And thou shalt bring his sons, and clothe them with coats: And thou shalt anoint them, as thou didst anoint their father that they may minister unto me in the priest's office: for their anointing shall surely be an everlasting priesthood throughout their generations. Thus did Moses: according to all that the Lord commanded him, so did he" (Exodus 40:11–16).*

Following their washing at sanctification, it became the responsibility of Aaron and his sons to continue the cleansing process in accordance with God's instructions. Scripture instructs the priests to wash their hands and feet. *"For Aaron and his sons shall wash their hands and their feet in water from it. When they go into the tabernacle of meeting, or when they come near the altar to minister, to burn an offering made by fire to the Lord, they shall wash with water, lest they die" (Exodus 30:19–20).*

The hands of a man speak of what he does; his service to God and man, the protection and provision for his family, and his occupation of work. Every duty the priests put their hands to was important ministry, and so their hands were required to be cleansed often. The feet of a man represent where he travels; they represent his life, his movement and his ways. The walk of the priest was required to be a holy walk, so their feet were also washed often.

The Spiritual Essence of the Bronze Laver

Since the brazen altar of sacrifice was the place where death occurred, it points to the sacrificial death of Jesus. The bronze laver, being filled with water, a major source of life, points to life through Jesus Christ. The shedding of blood speaks of life taken, but water speaks of life given. The water in the laver, with the spiritual power to cleanse and position one spiritually to minister before God, speaks of Jesus, who is the living, washing, Word of God that redeems believers and gives eternal life. *"I am crucified with Christ: nevertheless I live; yet not I, but Christ lives in me: and the life which I now live in the flesh I live by the faith of the Son of God, who loved me, and gave himself for me" (Galatians 2:20).*

Jesus said that we are cleansed by the washing of the water of his Word. Water brings life to the physical world and so, spiritual water, the Word of God, produces spiritual life. When Jesus met the woman at the well, he said to her: *"Whoever drinks of this well water will thirst again, but whoever drinks of the water that I shall give him will never thirst. The water that I shall give him will become in him a fountain of water springing up into everlasting life" (John 4:13).* When Jesus stood and cried, *"If any man thirst let him come to Me and drink," (John 7:37),* it was on the great day of the feast of tabernacles, the day when the Jewish leaders were pouring the water from the pool of Siloam onto the pavement of the temple, symbolizing that someday God will pour out the real water from heaven on his people as promised through the prophet Ezekiel. *"Then will I sprinkle clean water upon you, and ye shall be clean: from all your filthiness, and from all your idols, will I cleanse you. A new heart also will I give you, and a new spirit will I put within you: and I will take away the stony heart out of your flesh, and I will give you an heart of flesh. And I will put my spirit within you, and cause you to walk in my statutes, and ye shall keep my judgments, and do them" (Ezekiel 36:25–27).*

Then Ephesians 5 says: *"Husbands, love your wives, just as Christ also loved the church and gave himself for her, that he might sanctify and cleanse her with the washing of the water by the word" (Ephesians 5:25-26).* Jesus says in John: *"He who believes in me, as the scripture has said, out of his belly will flow Rivers of living water" (John 7:38).* So, those who embrace the sacrifice that Jesus made, become fountains, overflowing and always prepared to minister washing to others with the washing of the Word.

THE HOLY PLACE

Having completed our study of the outer court and its furnishings, we now make our entrance into the first section or compartment, of the tabernacle building, called the *Holy Place*. Here we begin our examination of the tabernacle's structural framework and its coverings. Because the structure contained both the Holy Place and the most Holy Place our examination of the Structure and its, coverings will necessarily apply to both compartments. Also, we will look at the furnishings and instruments located inside this first compartment called the Holy Place, including the golden lampstand, the table of shewbread, the shewbread itself, and the four vessels of pure gold that sat on the table with the shewbread. When the priests entered the Holy place they was leaving the outer court and entering the tabernacle structure through the door of the Holy Place, the first room of this two-room tent that was the main feature in the tabernacle complex. It was a rectangular structure measuring thirty cubits (45 feet) in length by ten cubits (15 feet) in height and breadth.

The Holy Place, where the priest set out the "bread of the presence" called the shewbread, was a room twenty cubits long by ten cubits wide and ten cubits in height (30 feet x 15 feet x 15 feet). Upright, wooden studs overlaid with gold, framed its four sides. This upright framework was covered by beautiful woven linen curtains with cherubim in the pattern that could be viewed through the front, sides, and ceiling of the entire structural framework. There were four golden pillars at the entrance and at the rear of this first compartment, at the rear of the Holy Place hung the *"Holy veil"*. Beyond the Holy veil was the second compartment called the *Holy of Holies,* where God sat on the mercy seat above the Ark of the Covenant. Here inside the Holy Place were the golden lampstand located on the left side of the room, the table of shewbread on the right side of the room; the golden altar of incense stood in the rear of this room just before the Holy veil. The entrance door of the Holy Place that was the door into the tabernacle structure is described in Exodus 26:36–37. *"And thou shalt make an hanging for the door of the tent, of blue, and purple, and scarlet, and fine twined linen, wrought with needlework. And thou shalt make for the hanging five pillars of shittim wood, and overlay them with gold, and their hooks shall be of gold: and thou shalt cast five sockets of brass for them."*

Only the priests, Aaron and his sons, could enter inside the tabernacle structure. The beautiful, skillfully woven, multicolored curtain, called the door, revealed the holiness of God, evidenced by the cherubim embroidered throughout this curtain; these cherubim always guard the holiness of God. The door to the Holy Place was ten cubits long by ten cubits wide. Also, the entrance gate to the outer court was twenty by five cubits, and the Holy veil entrance to the Holy of holies was ten cubits squared. It is interesting to note that the measurement of all three entrances of the tabernacle totaled one hundred cubits.

The door to the Holy Place had five pillars of acacia wood overlaid with gold, with five bronze sockets. Each pillar had a capital (crown) of gold (see Exodus 36:38). This gold-bronze mix is unusual. Recall that gold represents God's righteousness, while bronze represents judgment: *"The Lord reigneth; let the earth rejoice; let the multitude of isles be glad thereof. Clouds and darkness are round about him: righteousness and judgment are the habitation of his throne." (Psalm 97:1–2)*

The Table of Shewbread

"Thou shalt also make a table of shittim wood: two cubits shall be the length thereof, and a cubit the breadth thereof, and a cubit and a half the height thereof. And thou shalt overlay it with pure gold, and make thereto a crown of gold round about. And thou shalt make unto it a border of a hand breadth round about, and thou shalt make a golden crown to the border thereof round about. And thou shalt make for it four rings of gold, and put the rings in the four corners that are on the four feet thereof. Over against the border shall the rings be for places of the staves to bear the table. And thou shalt make the staves of shittim wood, and overlay them with gold, that the table may be borne with them. And thou shalt make the dishes thereof, and spoons thereof, and covers thereof, and bowls thereof, to cover withal: of pure gold shalt thou make them. And thou shalt set upon the table shewbread before me always." (Exodus 25:23–30). The purpose of the golden table was to hold the twelve cakes of shewbread made of fine flour. These twelve cakes were placed there in two rows of six, each cake representing one of the twelve tribes of Israel: *"And thou shalt take fine flour, and bake twelve cakes thereof: two tenth deals shall be in one cake. And thou shalt set them in two rows, six on a row, upon the pure table before the Lord. And thou shalt put pure frankincense upon each row that it may be on the bread for a memorial, even an offering made by fire unto the Lord. Every Sabbath he shall set it in order before the Lord continually, being taken from the children of Israel by an everlasting covenant. And it shall be Aaron's and his sons'; and they shall eat it in the holy place: for it is most holy unto him of the offerings of the Lord made by fire by a perpetual statute" (Leviticus 24:5–9).*

Josephus, the ancient historian indicates that the bread was unleavened. This bread is sometimes referred to as the shewbread, and sometimes as the "bread of the presence". Its literal meaning is "bread of the face" meaning the bread that set before the face of God continually.

This table of the shewbread is the first mention in the tabernacle of the word table. It points to the communion table. On the table with the shewbread were four vessels of pure gold, the bread-plates, the pans or spoons used to sprinkle the frankincense, the pitchers for liquid offerings, bowls, and the vessels containing the frankincense.

The Shewbread

"And thou shalt take fine flour, and bake twelve cakes thereof: two tenth deals shall be in one cake. And thou shalt set them in two rows, six on a row, upon the pure table before the Lord." The fine flour grown from the earth and baked signified the agony and suffering of Jesus on the cross. Unleavened means cleansed, or having nothing artificial pointed to His divine existance. Two tenth deals is a measurement meaning two-tenths of an ephah, which weighed thirteen and a half pounds, and the bread was sprinkled with pure frankincense. *"And thou shalt put pure frankincense upon each row, that it may be on the bread for a memorial, even an offering made by fire unto the Lord" (Leviticus 24:7).*

Every seventh or Sabbath day Aaron, the high priest, replaced the shewbread from the previous week with fresh hot loaves. The priests were allowed to eat the old loaves *while standing* in the Holy Place. The twelve loaves were of the same composition, size, and weight to show no partiality. The frankincense was also removed each week; it was a special oblation [offering to God].

According to Leviticus 22, if a priest was unclean, he could not eat of the shewbread. No layman or hired servant could eat of the shewbread. However, a purchased slave, or those born in Aaron's house, could eat. According to tradition, the priests held hands as they blessed the bread and as they passed it among themselves for fellowship. *"They shall be holy unto their God and not profane the name of their God: for the offerings of the Lord made by fire and the bread of their God, they do offer: therefore they shall be holy" (Leviticus 21:6).*

Although the bread was on a table, no priest could ever be seated at that table, or anyplace in the tabernacle. Priests always stood while they carried out their duties. There was no place to be seated, no provision for rest, because their work was never completed. They ministered redemption continuously, often to the same person time and time again. This differs from the ministry of Jesus Christ, who when he was sacrificed once for all, he sat down at the right hand of the father. *"And every priest standeth daily ministering and offering oftentimes the same sacrifices, which can never take away sins. But this man Jesus, after he had offered one sacrifice for sin forever, sat down on the right hand of God; from henceforth expecting till his enemies be made his footstool. For by one offering he hath perfected forever them that are sanctified" (Hebrews. 10:11–14).*

The Spiritual Essence of the Table of Shewbread

The table of shewbread was also referred to as the table of the bread of presence, because it sat before the presence of God, being naked before his glory and exposed continually to the mind of God. The twelve baked cakes of bread spoke of the twelve tribes of Israel's continued presence before God's face; this table and bread are also symbolic of the fact that the influence of God's presence is forever with his people. As the priests in the Holy Place joined together for the fellowship of eating the replaced bread, they became one among themselves. The church is instructed to break the bread that represents the body of the Lord and to drink the wine that represents his blood to become one with one another and one with Christ Jesus, who referred to himself as the bread of life.

The very nature of natural bread is to provide physical sustenance to the body; and as we consume and digest natural bread it becomes one with us. The very nature of the Word of God is to provide spiritual sustenance; as we embrace the Word it becomes one with our very nature. Just as the communion table always speaks of fellowship and intimacy with God and man, so the table of the shewbread points to the believer's intimacy with Jesus Christ, who gives us a new covenant built on better promises and has instructed us to partake of a blood-covenant meal that we might all be one in the spirit. *"For Christ is not entered into the holy places made with hands, which are the figures of the true; but into heaven itself, now to appear in the presence of God for us: Nor yet that he should offer himself often, as the high priest entereth into the holy place every year with blood of others; For then must he often have suffered since the foundation of the world: but now once in the end of the world hath he appeared to put away sin by the sacrifice of himself (Hebrews 9:24–26).* Also see John 6:35: *"And Jesus said unto them I am the bread of life: he that cometh to me shall never hunger; and he that believeth on me shall never thirst."*

Jesus had much to say about bread and life. Please read the following scriptures: *"I am the living bread which came down from heaven: if any man eats of this bread, he shall live forever: and the bread that I will give is my flesh, which I will give for the life of the world. The Jews therefore strove among themselves, saying, how can this man give us his flesh to eat? Then Jesus said unto them, verily, verily, I say unto you, except ye eat the flesh of the son of man, and drink his blood, ye have no life in you. Whoso eateth my flesh, and drinketh my blood, hath eternal life; and I will raise him up at the last day. For my flesh is meat indeed, and my blood is drink indeed, he that eateth my flesh, and drinketh my blood, dwelleth in me, and I in him. As the living father hath sent me, and I live by the father: so he that eateth me, even he shall live by me. This is that bread which came down from heaven: not as your fathers did eat manna, and are dead: he that eateth of this bread shall live forever"* (John 6:51–58). And then He took time to make clear distinction between spirit and the flesh: *"It is the Spirit who gives life; the flesh profits nothing. The words that I speak to you are spirit, and they are life"* (John 6:63).

Jesus Christ as great high priest on behalf of his people obliterated the sin-debt; His is an ever-finished redemptive work. His sacrifice was fully effective and completed work once and for all times. No earthly priest could ever be seated because his work was always unfinished the sins that were atoned needed to be atoned time and time again. After Jesus' great cry on the cross, "It is finished," Jesus Christ departed the sacrificial altar of Calvary and sat down at the right hand of Father God, where he ever makes intercessions *[divine interventions]* for you and me.

THE GOLDEN LAMPSTAND

God's instructions to Moses regarding the golden lampstand are given in the book of Exodus: *"And thou shalt make a candlestick of pure gold: of beaten work shall the candlestick be made: his (its) shaft and branches, his bowls, his knops, and his flowers, shall be of the same. And six branches shall come out of the sides of it; three branches of the candlestick out of the one side, and three branches of the candlestick out of the other side: Three bowls made like unto almonds, with a knop and a flower in one branch; and three bowls made like almonds in the other branch, with a knop and a flower: so in the six branches that come out of the candlestick and in the candlesticks shall be four bowls made like unto almonds, with their knops and their flowers. And there shall be a knop under two branches of the same, and a knop under two branches of the same, and a knop under two branches of the same, according to the six branches that proceed out of the candlestick. Their knops and their branches shall be of the same: all it shall be one beaten work of pure gold. And thou shalt make the seven lamps thereof: and they shall light the lamps thereof, that they may give light over against it. And the tongs thereof, and the snuff dishes thereof, shall be of pure gold. Of a talent of pure gold shall he make it, with all these vessels. And look that thou make them after their pattern, which was shewed thee in the mount"* (Exodus 25:31–40).

The golden lampstand was hammered from one piece of solid beaten gold, and weighed more than one hundred pounds. In the Hebrew language it is known as the Menorah. It stood on the south side of the Holy Place directly opposite the table of shewbread and illuminated this room without a window. The golden lampstand was a work of extraordinary beauty and consisted of three main parts: the base, the shaft, and the branches. Out of the base arose a vertical shaft, and from either side of the shaft sprang three branches, curving outward and upward. Each of the six branches held a cup, made like an open almond flower. The seven oil lamps, made to rest inside the flower petals, were like small bowls, and each of the opened petals of the flower held an oil lamp. The branches and the central shaft were skillfully decorated with that same open almond blossom design, with three on each branch and four on the center shaft. The decorations were exquisite and intricate and God commanded that only the most highly skilled craftsmen, anointed by the Holy Spirit, should make it. The word *almond* in the Hebrew language is associated with an awakening because the almond tree was the first tree to awaken and blossom following the sleep of winter. It spoke of the speedy and powerful process of light. The word light is often interpreted knowledge, understanding, or the believer's awakening to a deeper awareness of their redemption in Jesus Christ.

No measurements are given as to the exact size of the lampstand … who can measure the light of the Holy Place of God? A flax or linen wick was placed in the seven oil lamps resting in the flower petals; then they were lighted and the fire was to burn eternally. *"And thou shall command the children of Israel that they bring unto thee pure oil, olive, beaten for the light, to cause the lamps to burn continually" (Leviticus. 24:2).* The high priest was responsible for attending to the wick and replenished the pure beaten olive oil for the lamps each morning and evening. *"And Aaron shall burn thereon sweet incense every morning: when he dresseth the lamps, he shall burn incense upon it" (Exodus 30:7).*

"And thou shalt command the children of Israel, that they bring thee pure oil olive beaten for the light, to cause the lamp to burn always. In the tabernacle of the congregation without (outside) the veil, which is before the testimony (the testimony is a reference to the Ten Commandments written on two tablets of stone), Aaron and his sons shall order it from evening to morning before the Lord: it shall be a statute forever unto their generations on the behalf of the children of Israel" (Exodus 27:20–21).

The high priest alone trimmed and dressed the lamps. He alone was responsible for the light shining in the Holy Place. *"Outside the veil of the Testimony in the tabernacle of meeting, Aaron shall be in charge of it from evening until morning before the Lord continually; it shall be a statute forever in your generations" (Leviticus. 24:3).*

Whether people were, or were not, present in the Holy Place, all day and all night the seven lamps of the golden lampstand constantly illuminated the glory of the Holy Place; its light reflected directly and, some say, especially on the table of the shewbread immediately across the room as a reminder that the light of God's presence reflects in the world by those who are truly God's people.

The Spiritual Essence of the Golden Lampstand

Scripture, speaking of Jesus says: *"In him was life and the life was the light of men. And the light shines in the darkness, and the darkness did not comprehend it. There was a man sent from God, whose name was John. This man came for a witness, to bear witness of the Light, that all, through him might believe. He [John] was not that Light, but was sent to bear witness of that Light. That was the true Light which gives light to every man coming into the world that God is light and in him is no darkness at all" (John 1:4–9).*

When the apostle John says in John 1:5, *"And the light shineth in darkness; and the darkness comprehended it not,"* he was referring to the fact that Jesus came into the world to die for mankind and to teach truth about the kingdom of God, and the darkness of the world *[those with dimness of understanding]* did not comprehend, or appreciate the awesomeness of this message. Further, they did not understand that He, Jesus was the maker of the world. *"All things were made by him; and without him was not anything made that was made" (John 1:3).* However, he came to bring eternal life to all who will accept him. Since sinful man is in darkness, and apart from the privileges of salvation in Jesus Christ, they were unable to comprehend the truth that was revealed to those living their life in obedience to Jesus Christ and the laws of the kingdom of God.

As this golden lampstand illuminated the Holy Place and, in particular the table of shewbread, the spirit of God has been sent by Jesus to illuminate the mental darkness of mankind and introduce him to the spiritual life through Christ Jesus. John went on to say that Jesus was the true Light which makes available light [understanding] to all mankind. *"He was in the world, and the world was made by Him, and the world did not know him. He came to his own (the Jewish leaders), and his own did not receive him."* [Clarification: not all Jews rejected Jesus; many of his followers were Jews.] *"But to as many as received him, to them gave he the power to become sons of God, to those who were born, not of blood, nor of the will of the flesh, nor of the will of mankind, but of God" (John 1:9-13).* Human beings, apart from Jesus and the work of the Holy Spirit, are spiritually blind. Mankind cannot know God apart from Jesus and the power of the Holy Spirit. See 1 Corinthians: *"But the natural man receiveth not the things of the spirit of God: for they are foolishness unto him: neither can he know them, because they are spiritually discerned" (1 Corinthians 14).* Even if a human came face to face with God himself, without a renewed mind (full faith in the work and power of the Holy Spirit of God), they would be incapable of receiving the spiritual blessings that God desires for mankind because the darkness of this present world has made them blind to spiritual reality. See 2

Corinthians: *"But their minds were blinded: for until this day remaineth the same veil untaken away in the reading of the old testament; which veil is done away in Christ" (2 Corinthians 3:14).*

The golden lampstand speaks of our redeemer Jesus Christ of whom the messianic prophet Isaiah foretold long before he came to earth: *"There shall come forth a rod from the stem of Jesse, and a branch shall grow out of his roots. The spirit of the Lord shall rest upon him, the spirit of wisdom and understanding, the spirit of counsel and might, the spirit of knowledge and of the fear of the Lord" (Isaiah 11:1–2).* The golden lampstand also reminds us of Jesus as the redeeming light of the world. He said himself: *"As long as I am in the world, I am the light of the world" (John 9:5).* The book of Psalms also speaks about Jesus as the light. *"The Lord is my light and my salvation; whom shall I fear? The Lord is the strength of my life; of whom shall I be afraid" (Psalm 27:1).* Jesus as the Word gives light: *"Your Word is a lamp to my feet and a light to my path" (Psalm 119:105).* Then in Matthew, *"The people who sat in darkness have seen a great light, and upon those who sat in the region and shadow of death light has dawned" (Matthew 4:16).*

"And this is the condemnation [the basis for judgment against mankind], that the light has come into the world, and men loved darkness rather than light, because their deeds were evil. For everyone practicing evil hates the light and does not come to the light, lest his deeds should be exposed. But he who does the truth comes to the light, that his deeds may be clearly seen, that they have been done in God" (John 3:19–21). Further words of Jesus: *"Then Jesus spoke to them again, saying, I am the light of the world. He who follows me shall not walk in darkness, but have the light of life."* (John 8:12) The scriptures speaking about believers say the following: *"For you were sometimes darkness, but now you are light in the Lord. Walk as children of light" (Ephesians 5:8). "But you are a chosen generation a royal priesthood a holy nation his own special people, that you may proclaim the praises of him who called you out of darkness into his marvelous light." (1 Peter 2:9)*

"But if we walk in the light as he is in the light, we have fellowship with one another, and the blood of Jesus Christ his son cleanses us from all sin" (1 John 1:7) *"You are the light of the world; a city that is set on a hill cannot be hidden"* (Matthew 5:14). Jesus is the light of the world.

The Golden Altar of Incense

This golden altar of incense was located inside the Holy Place centered before the entrance to the Holy of holies, called the Holy veil. If one would take a straight-line eastward view from behind the altar of incense, back through the entrance door to the Holy Place, the three pieces of furniture located inside the Holy Place (the altar of incense, the table of showbread on the one side, and the golden lampstand on the other) would take on the form of the cross of Christ.

The altar of incense was made from acacia wood overlaid with pure gold, and it stood higher than any other article of furniture in the Holy Place: two cubits (3 feet) tall. It was one cubit square and it had around the top a crown of gold. It also had four horns, as did the brazen altar located in the outer courtyard. On each side there were golden rings to insert the poles for transporting it. The instructions for its construction as given to Moses by God are in Exodus: *"And thou shalt make an altar to burn incense upon: of shittim wood shalt thou make it. A cubit shall be the length thereof, and a cubit the breadth thereof; foursquare shall it be: and two cubits shall be the height thereof: the horns thereof shall be of the same. And thou shalt overlay it with pure gold, the top thereof, and the sides thereof round about, and the horns thereof; and thou shalt make unto it a crown of gold round about. And two golden rings shalt thou make to it under the crown of it, by the two corners thereof, upon the two sides of it shalt thou make it; and they shall be for places for the staves to bear it withal. And thou shalt make the staves of shittim wood, and overlay them with gold. And thou shalt put it before the veil that is by the ark of the testimony, before the mercy seat that is over the testimony, where I will meet with thee. And*

Aaron shall burn thereon sweet incense every morning: when he dresseth the lamps, he shall burn incense upon it. And when Aaron lighteth the lamps at even, he shall burn incense upon it, perpetual incense before the Lord throughout your generations. Ye shall offer no strange incense thereon, nor burnt sacrifice, nor meat offering; neither shall ye pour drink offering thereon. And Aaron shall make atonement upon the horns of it once in a year with the blood of the sin offering of atonements: once in the year shall he make atonement upon it throughout your generations: it is most holy unto the Lord" (Exodus 30:1–10).

Twice each day the priest, after he had tended the wicks and oil for the holy lamps, would offer to God by burning incense from this altar. Also, blood harvested from the sacrificial sin offerings was sprinkled on the horns of this altar. The incense was a mixture of three rich and very rare spices. These spices were blended with frankincense and beaten to a fine powder. The used of this formula by any private individual was totally forbidden; it was used only in the worship of God in the Holy Place. *"And the Lord said unto Moses, Take unto thee sweet spices, stacte, and onycha, and galbanum; these sweet spices with pure frankincense: of each shall there be a like weight: And thou shalt make it a perfume, a confection after the art of the apothecary, tempered together, pure and holy: And thou shalt beat some of it very small, and put of it before the testimony in the tabernacle of the congregation, where I will meet with thee: it shall be unto you most holy. And as for the perfume, which thou shalt make, ye shall not make to yourselves according to the composition thereof: it shall be unto thee holy for the Lord. Whosoever shall make like unto that, to smell thereto, shall even be cut off from his people" (Exodus 30:34–38).*

The spices added to the frankincense named above are made from all natural substances: *Stacte* is a powder from hardened drops of the fragrant resin found in the bark of the myrrh bush. *Onycha* is a powder from the thorny-shell covering of a clam-like mollusk that the Hebrews called "the aromatic shell" found in the Red Sea; and when this powder burned it would emit a penetrating aroma. The Red Sea is an isolated warm-water pocket of the Indian Ocean and is known for its peculiar subspecies of mollusks. *Galbanum* is a brownish, pungent resin that exudes from the lower part of the stem of the ferula plant. This herb *acetous*, a vinegar producing plant, found near the Mediterranean Sea, has thick stalks with yellow flowers, and fernlike green foliage. It has a musky, pungent smell and is valuable because it preserves the scent of mixed perfume and allows for its distribution over a long period of time. These spices or perfumes, as they are called, along with the frankincense, were burned to create a cloud to protect the high priests in his service before almighty God.

When these spices are mixed with the olive oil, they project a sense of comfort and self-assurance, compared to what believers experience when they encounter the revealing illuminating work of the Holy Spirit of Christ. Add to that combination the frankincense, which is symbolic of the sweetness of the prayers of the saints to the father, and you have the makings of the relationship-building encounter that occurs when humanity embraces Jesus Christ: the comforting power of the Holy Spirit, whom he left us as he departed earth, who makes us one with God. Jesus is speaking in John: *"And he that sent me is with me: the father hath not left me alone; for I do always those things that please him"* *(John 8:29).*

See and follow the instructions from the Apostle Paul, in Ephesians: *"And walk in love, as Christ also hath loved us, and hath given himself for us an offering and a sacrifice to God for a sweet-smelling savor" (Ephesians 5:2).* In Corinthians, again, the Apostle speaks of himself and his ministry team, who represent all believers when he says: *"For we are unto God a sweet savour of Christ, in them that are saved and in them that perish: To the one we are the savour of death unto death; and to the other the savour of life unto life, And who is sufficient for these things? For we are not as many, which corrupt the word of God: but as of sincerity, but as of God, in the sight of God speak we in Christ" (2 Corinthians 2:15–17).* When the incense was poured out on burning coals, it produced first, a cloud, and then a delightful aroma inside the Holy Place. It was an offering made for a person whose sins had been atoned by the blood of their sacrifice. A person who had atoned for their sin and been cleansed at the laver, could appreciate the further service of worship, to be done by the priest on his behalf, as the priest now took the blood of his personal sacrifice and performed service before God on his behalf.

The golden altar of incense speaks to us of the worship of Jesus Christ, the high priest and mediator for believers. It is only on the basis of his once-for-all, sacrificial blood shed on the altar of the cross at Golgotha, that real worship is made possible. The coals that lit the incense were carried from the brazen altar of burnt sacrifice to the altar of incense. Aaron's sons (the priests) would burn holy spices on the altar of incense numerous times a year, but on the Day of Atonement the high priest entered beyond the holy veil into the holy of holies, into the very presence of God. Because the scriptures point out that no man shall see God and live, the smoke-cloud created by the burning of incense would protect him as he ministered in the very presence of God. See Leviticus 16:12: *"And he shall take a censer full of burning coals of fire from off the altar before the Lord, and his hands full of sweet incense beaten small, and bring it within the veil."* The sweet incense was to continually burn on the golden altar of incense at all times. Notice that this altar of incense was just outside the veil to the Holy of holies, the dwelling place of God; it was before the throne of God.

The Spiritual Essence of the Golden Altar of Incense

The perpetual intercession made on behalf of mankind from the golden altar of incense speaks to us of the perpetual ministry of Jesus Christ, seated at the right hand of the father, ever making intercessions for you and me. His prayers never cease on our behalf. Jesus, who gave his own redeeming blood at the altar of the cross of Calvary, qualifies to intercede continually before the face of God. While the incense fueled by fire from this altar created a cloud of protection for the ministry of the high priest as he offered a sweet-smelling aroma pleasing to God, Jesus Christ, who is God manifested in the flesh, is King of kings, Lord of lords, the Alpha and the Omega, the beginning and the end, needs no such protection. He is able to continually minister on our behalf because he knows our weaknesses and failings: *"For we have not an high priest which cannot be touched with the feeling of our infirmities; but was in all points tempted like as we are, yet without sin" (Hebrews 4:15).* He prays, ever making intercessions for us always.

Please read the following scriptures for further understanding of the symbolism of this altar. About his current altar-prayer, Jesus said about believers: *"I pray for them: I pray not for the world, but for them which thou hast given me; for they are thine. And all mine are thine and thine are mine; and I am glorified in them" (John 17:9–10).* And in John 17:15 He says, *"I pray not that thou shouldest take them out of the world, but that thou shouldest keep them from the evil."*

The Lord talks to Peter saying, *"Simon, Simon, behold, Satan hath desired to have you, that he may sift you as wheat: But I have prayed for thee, that thy faith fail not: and when thou art converted, strengthen thy brethren" (Luke 22:31–32).* Scripture is replete with prayers similar to those prayed at this altar. *"Let my prayer be set forth before thee as incense; and the lifting up of my hands as the evening sacrifice" (Psalm 141:2).* *"Wherefore he is able also to save them to the uttermost that come unto God by him, seeing he ever liveth to make intercession for them" (Hebrews 7:25).* *"Likewise the spirit also helpeth our infirmities: for we know not what we should pray for, as we ought: but the spirit himself maketh intercession for us with groaning's which cannot be uttered. And he that searcheth the hearts knoweth what is the mind of the spirit, because he maketh intercession for the saints according to the will of God" (Romans 8:26–27).* *"Let us therefore come boldly unto the throne of grace that we may obtain mercy, and find grace to help in the time of need" (Hebrews 4:16).* And it continues, *"Who is he that condemneth? It is Christ that died, yea rather, that is risen again, who is even at the right hand of God, who also maketh intercession for us" (Romans 8:34). "But we will give ourselves continually to prayer and to the ministry of the word" (Acts 6:4). "By him therefore let us offer the sacrifice of praise to God continually that is, the fruit of our lips giving thanks to his name" (Hebrews 13:15). "And when he had taken the book, the four beasts and four and twenty elders fell down before the lamb, having every one of them harps, and golden vials full of odors, which are the prayers of saints." (Revelation 5:8). "And another angel came and stood at the altar, having a golden censer; and there was given unto him much incense, that he should offer it with the prayers of all saints upon the golden altar which was before the throne. And the smoke of the incense, which came with the prayers of the saints, ascended up before God out of the angel's hand" (Revelation 8:3–4).*

The perpetual priestly-ministry proceeding from the golden altar of incense is a foreshadowing of the perpetual ministry of Jesus as our intercessor, whose prayers to God on our behalf never cease.

THE HOLY OF HOLIES

The Holy of holies was literally where God dwelled on earth. Its only access was through the *Holy veil.* As with all parts of the tabernacle, God's instructions to Moses regarding the Holy of holies and its entrance were no less exacting. *"And thou shalt make a veil of blue, purple and scarlet, and of fine twined linen of cunning work: with cherubim shall it be made: And thou shalt hang it upon four pillars of shittim wood overlaid with gold: their hooks shall be of gold, upon the four sockets of silver. And thou shalt hang up the veil under the taches, that thou mayest bring in thither within the veil the ark of the testimony: and the veil shall divide unto you between the holy place and the most holy. And thou shalt put the mercy seat upon the ark of the testimony (Ark of the Covenant) in the most holy place" (Exodus 26:31–34).*

The Holy veil separated man and all his activities from God. It was hung with golden hooks from four gold-covered pillars and was made of acacia wood that rested upon sockets of silver. The word *"veil"* means to hide or separate; and notice, this veil was made with the same colors as the decorated curtains visible inside the Holy Place and the Holy of holies. It was made of finely spun white linen dyed blue, purple, and scarlet and woven into it were the richly adorned figures of cherubim. It was also referred to as *"the curtain of the testimony"*, a reference to the tables of the Ten Commandments stored inside. The veil could never be touched, except by the high priest once a year when he entered there to sprinkle blood on the mercy seat on the Day of Atonement to atone for the sins of the nation of Israel. In fact, God gave Moses instructions that Aaron, the high priest at the time, was not to enter the Holy of holies on any casual basis: *"And the Lord said unto Moses, Speak unto Aaron thy brother, that he come not at all times into the holy of holies within the veil before the mercy seat, which is upon the ark; that he die not: for I will appear in the cloud upon the mercy seat"* (Leviticus 16:2).

The Colors

The question is raised from time to time as we teach this subject, where, in the wilderness, did the Hebrew people find these various colors, of blue, purple, and scarlet, so prominently mentioned as being woven into or embroidered on the fine white linen in this history? Well come and see:

The Color Blue

Historians have said that the blue color was to represent heaven. The Hebrew word used in the Bible to denote this special blue is *tekhelet*, a blue dye mentioned 48 times in the Hebrew Bible. The Talmud says the dye of *tekhelet* was produced from a marine creature known as the *ḥillazon*. We are told this brilliant dye was excreted from this marine mollusk. In English parlance, it is generally accepted that the color came from shellfish; this bright color is always mentioned first and many theologians believe the color blue here, represents our earthly sky and is symbolic of heaven. We know that our Lord was heavenly in his origin: *"In the beginning was the Word (Jesus), and the Word was with God, and the Word was God. The same was in the beginning with God. All things were made by him; and without him was not anything made that was made. (John 1:1-3)* Also see: *"He that cometh from above is above all: he that is of the earth is earthy, and speaketh of the earth: he that cometh from heaven is above all." (John 3:31).*

The Color Purple

The Hebrews made this color by mixing blue and scarlet together. This deep red-purple color was kingly, a color of royalty. We find a story in the book of Judges that speaks of the kingly origin of purple: *"And the weight of the golden earrings that he requested was a thousand and seven hundred shekels of gold; beside ornaments, and collars, and purple raiment that was on the kings of Midian, and beside the chains that were about their camels' necks" (Judges 8:26).*

The mixing of blue and scarlet produced the kingly color purple, which characterizes Jesus as King of kings and Lord of lords. However, we notice that scarlet, one of the colors in this mix, points to blood, death, sacrifice, and things earthy. As purple is a combination of both blue and scarlet, it is said that purple is symbolic of Jesus Christ as both God and man. He is God, and he took upon himself the likeness of sinful flesh, thereby embracing the nature of both God and the human.

The Color Scarlet

The color scarlet speaks of sacrifice. It was derived from an Eastern insect (a worm) that infested certain trees. The worms were gathered, crushed, dried, and ground to a powder, which produced a brilliant, crimson hue. Sacrifice characterizes Christ in his sufferings at Calvary. Jesus took upon himself a body of flesh and blood, and voluntarily died the death of crucifixion giving his life as ransom for us all.

The Cherubim

God's instructions to Moses regarding these prominently mentioned cherubim: *"And you shall make two cherubim of gold; of hammered work you shall make them at the two ends of the mercy seat. Make one cherub at one end, and the other cherub at the other end; you shall make the cherubim at the two ends of it of one piece with the mercy seat. And the cherubim shall stretch out their wings above, covering the mercy seat with their wings, and they shall face one another; the faces of the cherubim shall be toward the mercy seat" (Exodus 25:18–20).*

The cherubim represent the righteous of the government of God and are the protectors of God's righteous judgment. *"And the Lord God said, behold, the man is become as one of us, to know good and evil: and now, lest he put forth his hand, and take also of the tree of life, and eat, and live forever: therefore the Lord God sent him forth from the garden of Eden, to till the ground from whence he was taken. So he drove out the man; and he placed at the east of the Garden of Eden cherubim, and a flaming sword, which turned every way, to keep the way of the tree of life" (Genesis 3:22–24).* The cherubim, as guardians of God's holiness, are positioned always with their faces toward the mercy seat. God's destruction of Israel, in its times of disobedience, was averted because the cherubim continuously had in view the sacrificial blood sprinkled on the mercy seat.

The Four Pillars of the Holy Veil

The four strong pillars that supported the *Holy veil* were kept secure by the foundation and strength of their sockets, pegs and cords. This foundation points to Jesus as the believer's dependable foundation. *"For other foundation can no man lay than that is laid, which is Jesus Christ. Now if any man build upon this foundation gold, silver, precious stones, wood, hay, stubble; Every man's work shall be made manifest: for the day shall declare it, because it shall be revealed by fire; and the fire shall try every man's work of what sort it is. If any man's work abides which he hath built thereupon, he shall receive a reward" (1 Corinthians 3:11–14).*

The Holy veil was the only way into God's presence in the tabernacle;

likewise today, the only way into the presence of God is through the veil of the body of Jesus Christ. The true meaning of this veil is found in a brief statement by the Apostle Paul: *"the veil, that is to say, His flesh"* *(Hebrew 10:20).*

The Spiritual Essence of the Holy Veil

The veil is symbolic of the flesh of Jesus Christ. *"Having therefore, brethren, boldness to enter into the holiest by the blood of Jesus, By a new and living way, which he hath consecrated for us, through the veil, that is to say, his flesh" (Hebrews 10:19–20).* Now, all mankind can enter in [come to God] by the blood of Jesus Christ. All mankind is granted opportunity to accept [believe and embrace] the work that Jesus did on the cross of Calvary, and without human or earthly intermediary but by the spirit, go directly into the presence of God. Intercession is continually being made by Jesus Christ leaving no further need for intercession by a human priest, pastor or any earthly human. Believers can approach God through the rent (torn) veil that is Christ's broken body. Remember, the moment the spear was thrust into His side on his cross of crucifixion, the veil of the old tabernacle was torn, ripped from top to bottom, announcing that the way was opened to the throne room of God to all who believe in the savior's work on the cross. Jesus suffered to the point of death, on a Roman cross, that we might have free access directly to the father.

Scripture tells us that he died for the joy that was set before him, the joy of seeing millions upon millions of souls released from the grasp of the enemy. In other words, He was betrothed to those who would believe on his name; he promised to become one with them as in a marriage arrangement; by assuming responsibility for their outstanding debt by shedding his blood as payment for their sin-debt. It was the only way sinners could become legally unencumbered and free to be the bride of Christ, wedded to him for eternity. *"Looking unto Jesus the author and finisher of our faith; who for the joy that was set before him endured the cross, despising the shame, and is set down at the right hand of the throne of God" (Hebrews 12:2).* The veil being torn in two speaks of the flesh of Jesus Christ being torn from his body to make our access to his glory possible. *"Having therefore, brethren, boldness to enter into the holiest by the blood of Jesus, by a new and living way, which he hath consecrated for us, through the veil, that is to say, his flesh; and having an high priest over the house of God; let us draw near with a true heart in full assurance of faith, having our hearts sprinkled from an evil conscience, and our bodies washed with pure water" (Hebrews 10:19–22).* The writer of Matthew says this: *"And, behold, the veil of the temple was rent in twain [two] from the top to the bottom; and the earth did quake, and the rocks rent" (Matthew 27:51).* The pathway to the presence of God was opened and all who will accept [believe] that Jesus Christ's death on the cross opened access through his own flesh, are now invited to: *"Come boldly to the throne of grace that we may obtain mercy, and find grace to help in the time of need" (Hebrews 4:16).*

THE ARK OF THE COVENANT

Beyond the Holy veil, inside the Holy of holies, we find the Ark of the Covenant. *"And they shall make an ark of shittim wood: two cubits and a half shall be the length thereof, and a cubit and a half the breadth thereof, and a cubit and a half the height thereof. And thou shalt overlay it with pure gold, within and without shalt thou overlay it, and shalt make upon it a crown of gold round about. And thou shalt cast four rings of gold for it, and put them in the four corners thereof; and two rings shall be in the one side of it, and two rings in the other side of it. And thou shalt make staves of shittim wood, and overlay them with gold. And thou shalt put the staves into the rings by the sides of the ark that the ark may be borne with them. The staves shall be in the rings of the ark: they shall not be taken from it. And thou shalt put into the ark the testimony which I shall give thee. And thou shalt make a mercy seat of pure gold: two cubits and a half shall be the length thereof, and a cubit and a half the breadth thereof. And thou shalt make two cherubim of gold; of beaten work shalt thou make them, in the two ends of the mercy seat. And make one cherub on the one end, and the other cherub on the other end: even of the mercy seat shall ye make the cherubim on the two ends thereof. And the cherubim shall stretch forth their wings on high, covering the mercy seat with their wings, and their faces shall look one to another; toward the mercy seat shall the faces of the cherubim be. And thou shalt put the mercy seat above upon the ark; and in the ark thou shalt put the testimony that I shall give thee. And there I will meet with thee, and I will commune with thee from above the mercy seat, from between the two cherubim which are upon the ark of the testimony, of all things which I will give thee in commandment unto the children of Israel" (Exodus 25:10–22).*

Inside this ten cubits square chamber, the Holy of Holies located behind the Holy veil, is the Ark of the Covenant, the most sacred piece of furniture in the entire tabernacle structure. The cover, the top or lid of the ark, was known as the *mercy seat* where God dwelled as he lived among his people on earth; and although it is often referred to as a separate piece of furniture, *the mercy seat* was one with the ark. The precise location of the Ark marked the center of the overall camp, meaning the individual tribal tent-dwellings that surrounded the tabernacle complex. Also, the cloud that appeared by day and the pillar of fire that appeared at night were positioned directly above the Ark and its mercy seat, which was located in the most western portion of the tabernacle structure. Inside the Ark were three items of memorial value to the Israelites: they were the second set of two tablets of the Ten Commandments, a golden pot of manna, and Aaron's rod that budded. Remember, Moses had broken the first set of the tablets of the Ten Commandments upon returning form meeting with God in the mountain and finding that the children of Israel had violated their covenant with God with the golden calf incident (see Exodus 32:1-4 forward). God by his grace renewed the covenant and wrote a second set of tablets containing the Ten Commandments, and He ordered that this enduring record of the unbroken covenant between God and the people of Israel, be deposited inside the Holy Ark. Thus, the ark is called the Ark of the Covenant. There was also a Book of the Covenant, which dealt at length with other aspects of God's laws and procedures. This book was kept alongside, but outside of the ark. The jar contained an omer (24 liters, or 3.7 quarts) of manna (see Hebrews 9:4) as a memorial of God's provision of food for the nation of Israel during the wilderness journey: *"And Moses said, This is the thing which the Lord commandeth, fill an omer of it to be kept for your generations; that they may see the bread wherewith I have fed you in the wilderness, when I brought you forth from the land of Egypt. And Moses said unto Aaron, Take a pot, and put an omer full of manna therein, and lay it up before the Lord, to be kept for your generations" (Exodus 16:32–33).* This manna, which served as bread for the Israelites during their journey in the desert, is a type of Christ, who is the living bread for believers, which came down from heaven. *"This is the bread which cometh down from heaven, that believers may eat thereof, and not die. I am the living bread which came down from heaven: if any man eats of this bread, he shall live forever: and the bread that I will give is my flesh, which I will give for the life of the world" (John 6:50–51).*

The third item, Aaron's rod that budded, blossomed and bore almonds in a single night, had been used to settle a leadership dispute among the Israeli tribes. It confirmed God's choice of Aaron and the house of Levi as priestly leaders for the entire Israeli camp. *"And Moses laid up the rods before the Lord in the tabernacle of witness. And it came to pass, that on the morrow Moses went into the tabernacle of witness; and, behold, the rod of Aaron for the house of Levi was budded, and brought forth buds, and bloomed blossoms, and yielded almonds" (Numbers 17:7–8 and forward).*

Also, this 2½ x 1½-cubit, rectangular, wooden chest covered by the mercy seat is where the cherubim sat and faced each other with outstretched wings. It is where the sacrificial blood was sprinkled on the mercy seat, between these two judgment angels; and when they saw the sacrificial blood the wrath of God was stayed.

The Ark of the Covenant was overlaid with pure gold and had a gold crown. It was the only piece of furniture made by Moses, himself. *"At that time the Lord said unto me, hew thee two tables of stone like unto the first, and come up unto me into the mount, and make thee an ark of wood. And I will write on the tables the words that were in the first tables, which thou brakest, and thou shalt put them in the ark. And I made an ark of shittim wood, and hewed two tables of stone like unto the first, and went up into the mount, having the two tables in mine hand. And he wrote on the tables, according to the first writing, the Ten Commandments, which the Lord spake unto you in the mount out of the midst of the fire in the day of the assembly: and the Lord gave them unto me. And I turned myself and came down from the mount, and put the tables in the ark which I had made; and there they be, as the Lord commanded me" (Deuteronomy 10:1–5).*

The molding or crown around the top is pronounced in the Hebrew language "rim" a common word for us today. It should be noted that the word to describe this molding is different than the word used for the crowns on the table of shewbread and the altar of incense. The Ark of the Covenant was also where God's justice and judgment toward sin was satisfied as the High priest sprinkled the sacrificial blood of all the people once a year and it is referred to often in the Old Testament. *"And there I will meet with you, and I will speak with you from above the mercy seat, from between the two cherubim which are on the ark of the testimony, about everything which I will give you in commandment to the children of Israel" (Exodus 25:22).*

Again the scriptures are replete with how and where the Ark of the Covenant is referred to elsewhere in our bible. *"Then Joshua spoke to the priest, saying, take up the Ark of the Covenant and cross over before the people. So they took up the Ark of the Covenant and went before the people" (Joshua 3:6). "And it shall come to pass, as soon as the soles of the feet of the priests who bear the ark of the Lord, of all the earth, shall rest in the waters of the Jordan that the waters of the Jordan shall be cut off, the waters that come down from upstream, and they shall stand as a heap" (Joshua 3:13). "And when the men of Ashdod saw how it was, they said, 'The ark of the God of Israel must not remain with us, for his hand is harsh toward us and dagon our god'" (1 Samuel 5:7). "Now therefore arise, O Lord God, to your resting place, you and the ark of your strength. Let your priests, O Lord God, be clothed with salvation, and let your saints rejoice in goodness" (1 Chronicles 6:41). "Then he said to the Levites who taught all Israel, who were holy to the Lord: 'Put the holy ark in the house which Solomon the son of David, king of Israel, built. It shall no longer be a burden on your shoulders. Now serve the Lord your God and his people Israel'" (2 Chronicles 35:3).*

THE COVERINGS OF THE TABERNACLE

Now we study the tabernacle coverings that covered both the Holy Place and the Most Holy Place, they are compartments of the same building. The structure had four coverings: the first was linen, the second was goats' hair, the third was rams' skin dyed red, and the fourth was badgers' skin. The badger skin, a dull and unattractive covering, was visible to the outside view of the tabernacle. Here, as elsewhere, reading the instructions God gave to Moses significantly helps our understanding. *"Moreover thou shalt make the tabernacle with ten curtains of fine twined linen, of blue, and purple, and scarlet: with cherubim of cunning work shalt thou make them. The length of one curtain shall be eight and twenty cubits, and the breadth of one curtain four cubits: and every one of the curtains shall have one measure. The five curtains shall be coupled together one to another; and other five curtains shall be coupled one to another. And thou shalt make loops of blue upon the edge of the one curtain from the selvedge in the coupling; and likewise shalt thou make in the uttermost edge of another curtain, in the coupling of the second. Fifty loops shalt thou make in the one curtain, and fifty loops shalt thou make in the edge of the curtain that is in the coupling of the second; that the loops may take hold one of another. And thou shalt make fifty taches of gold, and couple the curtains together with the taches: and it shall be one tabernacle.*

And thou shalt make curtains of goats' hair to be a covering upon the tabernacle: eleven curtains shalt thou make. The length of one curtain shall be thirty cubits, and the breadth of one curtain four cubits: and the eleven curtains shall be all of one measure. And thou shalt couple five curtains by themselves and six curtains by themselves, and shalt double the sixth curtain in the forefront of the tabernacle. And thou shalt make fifty loops on the edge of the one curtain that is outmost in the coupling, and fifty loops in the edge of the curtain which coupleth the second. And thou shalt make fifty taches of brass, and put the taches into the loops, and couple the tent together, that it may be one. And the remnant that remaineth of the curtains of the tent, the half curtain that remaineth, shall hang over the backside of the tabernacle. And a cubit on the one side, and a cubit on the other side of that which remaineth in the length of the curtains of the tent, it shall hang over the sides of the tabernacle on this side and on that side, to cover it. And thou shalt make a covering for the tent of rams' skins dyed red, and a covering above of badgers' skins" (Exodus 26:1–14).

The Fine White Linen Covering

The first covering made of fine white twined linen, rested directly on the framework of the tabernacle structure; it was finely twisted and woven together with blue, purple, and scarlet materials according to God's instructions. This extravagantly beautiful curtain was decorated with skillfully embroidered figures of cherubim. These embroidered cherubim figures were found on this curtain and the veil. Since this curtain covered the entire structure, whether a priest was in the Holy Place or the Holy of holies, these cherubim were visible to be viewed through the structural framework of the building. The cherubim, whose main responsibility was to guard the Holiness of God, were amazingly powerful spiritual beings and, because of their spiritual significance, God instructed that they be embroidered on this first innermost curtain.

So, as the priests ministered in the Holy Place, these images of the cherubim were visible above them and all around them. The cherubim were a visual reminder of the holiness of God and they continually reminded the priests of the holiness and significance of their work: *"For I am the Lord your God: ye shall therefore sanctify yourselves, and ye shall be holy; for I am holy: neither shall ye defile yourselves with any manner of creeping thing that creepeth upon the earth. For I am the Lord that bringeth you up out of the land of Egypt, to be your God: ye shall therefore be holy, for I am holy" (Leviticus 11:44–45).*

This first beautiful linen covering with its cherubim gave form to the tabernacle. As it was placed over the framework, the tabernacle became one structure. This sizable covering was actually made of ten curtains coupled together. Each one of the smaller curtains was twenty-eight cubits, or forty-two feet long, by four cubits wide, and coupled together with the others, so one single length, was hung over the roof and down the sides of the framework to the place where it was one cubit or 18 inches short of the ground on either side. Remember, God said: *"And thou shalt make fifty taches of gold, and couple the curtains together with the taches: and it shall be one tabernacle" (Exodus 26:6).* To make this overall curtain more manageable, five curtains (half of the smaller curtains) were joined together yielding two larger units, each, twenty-eight by twenty cubits. In order to couple these curtains together, fifty loops of blue thread were sewn on the side of one curtain, and the same on the other curtain and fifty clasps of gold attached to the other side of the curtains. These attachments were used to join the curtains to each other in sequence per God's instruction to make one tabernacle.

This language of *"bringing together to make them one"* is familiar. Jesus used these words when he prayed for his followers: *"Neither pray I for these alone, but for them also which shall believe on me through thy word; That they all may be one; as thou, father, art in me, and I in thee, that they also may be one in us: that the world may believe that thou hast sent me. And the glory which thou gavest me I have given them; that they may be one, even as we are one" (John 17:20–22).* Just as there was no separation or drawing apart of the curtains covering the tabernacle, so there should be no separation or drawing apart of the body of Christ; his church is also instructed to be one inseparable body.

The Goats' Hair Covering

This second covering was made of goats' hair and overlaid the first covering. It needed to be slightly larger in size and was made from black goats' hair woven together. Instead of starting with ten narrow curtains, there were eleven and each of them measured eleven by thirty by four cubits. It was two cubits longer than the first to allow it to reach down to the ground, and entirely cover the first curtain. Six of these curtains of goats' hair were joined to make one large curtain, and the remaining five were joined to form the second curtain: *"And thou shalt couple five curtains by themselves and six curtains by themselves, and shalt double the sixth curtain in the forefront of the tabernacle" (Exodus 26:9).* These two larger curtains were then united in a similar way as the first curtain, but since this second curtain was less precious than the linen curtain, which directly overlaid the tabernacle structure, the clasps holding the fifty loops were made of bronze and not of gold.

This principle was the same throughout the entire tabernacle. The farther you moved from the Holy of Holies, the less valuable were the materials used. The lesson here is that in the presence of God exist all the positive qualities of life such as beauty, purity, power, peace, prosperity, rest, and salvation, all represented by gold. As one's lifestyle moves away from God as the center of their existence, the greater the influence of the world with its struggles, sufferings, unrest, shortages and judgment, represented by bronze. The entire length of the completed second curtain was forty-four cubits or 66 feet, by thirty cubits, 45 feet. Some of the length was used to make a fold across the top above the entrance of the tabernacle; its length was also used for overlapping the under-curtain around the sides and at the back of the tent. This goats' hair covering was draped in such a way that its attachments did not coincide with the attachments of the first curtain, avoiding any noise that might come from metal against metal in windy conditions.

The Covering of Rams' Skins Dyed Red

The third covering was made of rams' skins dyed red. It was the first of two weatherproof coverings. *"You shall also make a covering of rams' skins dyed red for the tent, and a covering of badger skins above that" (Exodus 26:14).* As we remember from Genesis chapter 22, a ram from the bush was used as the sacrifice in the account of Abraham and Isaac. Also, red represents the shed blood for the atonement in the tabernacle and for salvation in the New Testament. I found no measurements given for this covering.

The Badgers' Skins Covering

The fourth covering was made of badgers' skins and no measurements were given for this covering. The Hebrew lexicon word for badger is *tachash*. This word may refer to a badger or a "dugong" or sea cow. The dugong was an aquatic mammal previously found along the shores of the Red Sea, which is now almost extinct. As we see, the tabernacle coverings progress from the beautiful and spiritually significant, to the practical, and less attractive. We see the pattern from the first covering made of the finest white linen woven with blue, purple and scarlet, decorated with cherubim; to the unattractive, but protective, badger skin covering the outside of the tabernacle structure. This final cover of badger skins was far from beautiful. But as with everything in the kingdom of God, the deeper we search for the truth of God's original intent, the nearer we are drawn to his beauty, splendor, and a true understanding of the depth of his spirituality.

The Spiritual Essence of the Tabernacle Coverings

Each of the Tabernacle coverings points to Jesus Christ. The first innermost of the coverings with its beautiful colors and cherubim woven into the fine white linen represents the righteousness of God. Jesus Christ took on the sins of the world and paved the way for all humanity to become the righteousness of God. *"For he hath made him to be sin for us, who knew no sin; that we might be made the righteousness of God in him" (2 Corinthians 5:21)*

The second covering of goats' hair tells us that an innocent animal gave its life in order for its skin to be used, pointing to Jesus Christ as our substitutionary sacrifice who gave his life and paid the sin debt for all mankind. *"Therefore doth my Father love me, because I lay down my life, that I might take it again. No man taketh it from me, but I lay it down of myself. I have power to lay it down, and I have power to take it again. This commandment have I received of my Father" (John 10:17-18).*

The third covering of rams' skins dyed red, symbolizing blood, reminds us of Jesus as our substitutionary sacrifice, our lamb slain before the foundation of the world. This covering also reminds us of the ram that appeared suddenly and became the substitute sacrifice for Isaac, when his father Abraham in obedience to God lifted the knife to sacrifice his son. Read this historical scriptural record at Genesis chapter 22.

The last covering made of badger skins had an unattractive outward appearance, yet was so essential to the protection and covering of the Old Testament Tabernacle. Jesus was a Jewish man with nothing especially attractive about him that would make one think he was the King of kings or Lord of lords. The scriptures seem to say he was not necessarily the most attractive of men, today the value of His work to humankind is recognized universally as immeasurable. Without the protection of the badger skin cover to protect it from the elements, the tabernacle would have suffered exposure to the elements and deterioration. Any human being absent Jesus Christ suffers a measure of exposure to the devils devises and needless deterioration. Remember Isaiah's writings: *"For he shall grow up before him as a tender plant, and as a root out of a dry ground: he hath no form, nor comeliness; and when we shall see him, there is no beauty that we should desire him. He is despised and rejected by men, a man of sorrows and acquainted with grief. And we hid, as it were, our faces from him; he was despised, and we did not esteem him"* (Isaiah 53:2). However, to the wise among us, He is esteemed beyond what thoughts, ideas or words can express. Selah.

Moving the Tabernacle

When the tabernacle was finished according to the plans God gave Moses, God sent his spirit as a cloud during the day and as a pillar of fire at night. Whenever the spirit of God moved, the Israelites led by the movement of God would move the tabernacle. When it was time to relocate the tabernacle, the building and all its furnishings and utensils were taken down, disassembled, and moved to wherever God's spirit settled, as indicated by the cloud, and set up, reassembled, in the new location where God had led them. God consecrated the altar of incense, located inside the Holy Place before the Holy veil, as Most Holy and its contents could only be touched or handled by the priest. *"And there I will meet with the children of Israel, and the tabernacle shall be sanctified by my glory. And I will sanctify the tabernacle of the congregation, and the altar: I will sanctify also both Aaron and his sons, to minister to me in the priest's office. And I will dwell among the children of Israel, and will be their God. And they shall know that I am the Lord their God, that brought them forth out of the land of Egypt, that I may dwell among them: I am the Lord their God"* (Exodus 29:43–46).

God had instructed Moses at the beginning of the construction of the tabernacle as to the duties of all the sons of Levi, priests and non-priests alike, regarding the movement of the tabernacle. *"And when*

Aaron and his sons have made an end of covering the sanctuary, and all the vessels of the sanctuary, as the camp is to set forward [move]; after that, the sons of Kohath shall come to bear it: but they shall not touch any holy thing, lest they die. These things are the burden of the sons of Kohath in the tabernacle of the congregation" (Numbers 4:15).

Discerning the spirit and movement of God was essential then, and is essential for today's church, which sometimes is stuck in a place where God has departed. While God never changes, He does still move.

Why Study the Tabernacle?

Many people ask, *"Why study the Tabernacle of Moses?"* Again, it is good for us to remember the words of Proverbs: *"It is the glory of God to conceal a thing: but the honour of kings is to search out a matter"* (Proverbs 25:2). The scriptures instruct all mankind to search all of scripture, including scripture about this tabernacle, assuming nothing, but knowing it has pleased God in his glory to conceal eternal truths in His word. It has become the sacred duty of believers, who are made kings and priests of God, to search out these truths, that we might more fully understand and embrace them as instructions to live our lives by and accurately teach those who would come to God. See Revelation: *"And from Jesus Christ, who is the faithful witness, and the first begotten of the dead, and the prince of the kings of the earth. Unto him that loved us, and washed us from our sins in his own blood, And hath made us kings and priests unto God and his Father; to him be glory and dominion for ever and ever. Amen"* (Revelation 1:5-6) Also see: *"And they sung a new song, saying, Thou art worthy to take the book, and to open the seals thereof: for thou wast slain, and hast redeemed us to God by thy blood out of every kindred, and tongue, and people, and nation; And hast made us unto our God kings and priests: and we shall reign on the earth"* (Revelation 5:9–10). Then notice 1 Peter 2:5-9: *"Ye also, as lively stones, are built up a spiritual house, an holy priesthood, to offer up spiritual sacrifices, acceptable to God by Jesus Christ. But ye are a chosen generation, a royal priesthood, an holy nation, a peculiar people; that ye should shew forth the praises of him who hath called you out of darkness into his marvellous light."*

The writers of the New Testament refer on a regular basis to the Old Testament writings of the law, the prophets, and the Psalms. Without a basic understanding of this Old Testament Tabernacle, much of the New Testament's language will have no real meaning or basis in truth for the New Testament reader. The revelation found in the study of the Tabernacle of Moses is included in the pronouncement in 2 Timothy: *"All scripture is given by inspiration of God, and is profitable for doctrine, for reproof, for correction, for instruction in righteousness: it also, is given by inspiration of God and is profitable for doctrine, for reproof, for correction, and for instruction in righteousness." (2 Timothy 3:16).*

We study the Tabernacle because knowledge of this Old Testament phenomenon, its furnishings, instruments, people, and ceremonies, will equip seekers of truth to comprehend much of the spiritual language used in our modern-day Bibles. This tabernacle was a shadow of good things to come, a reference to the work of the coming savior Jesus Christ. However, it would take his shed blood to save the world. This old tabernacle was a forerunner for his coming. *"Which was a figure for the time then present, in which were offered both gifts and sacrifices, that could not make him that did the service perfect, as pertaining to the conscience; Which stood only in meats and drinks, and divers washings, and carnal ordinances, imposed on them until the time of reformation. But Christ being come an high priest of good things to come, by a greater and more perfect tabernacle, not made with hands, that is to say, not of this building; neither by the blood of goats and calves, but by his own blood he entered in once into the holy place, having obtained eternal redemption for us" (Hebrews 9: 9–12).*

It is my heart's desire that every believer, indeed every person, would understand that symbolism is a principle of spiritual study and scripture interpretation. The principle is this: it is the purpose of the symbol or shadow to chaperone or escort us to the substance; it is the purpose of prophetic announcements to lead us to recognize and understand the fulfillment of prophecy; it is the purpose of the type of a thing to bring us to the antitype. He who will study the shadow of a thing and understand the prophecy of a thing, and truly comprehend the type of a thing, is much more likely to benefit when the real thing comes. The Tabernacle was a shadow. Its reason for existence was to point us to the real. The shadow of a thing has no reality in and of itself. It can only point to the real, the authentic, from which the shadow was casted. On a warm day one may enjoy the shade of a tree, the branches may provide shade some distance from the tree; but if you follow the shade of that tree it will lead you to the trunk of the tree and finally to the tree.

Further, there is a principle of God's kingdom that applies here. *"Howbeit that was not first which is spiritual, but that which is natural; and afterward that which is spiritual. The first man is of the earth, earthy; the second man is the Lord from heaven; Adam, the first man, was made from the dust of the earth, while Christ, the second man of the spirit" (1 Corinthians 15:46–47).*

ATONEMENT VS. SALVATION

Understanding why and how God used the Tabernacle to create a way for lost, disobedient mankind to regain their position of righteousness, and how the precious gift of salvation evolved through the examples of substitution, sacrifice, bloodshed, and the ordinances and commandments of God demonstrated in this Old Testament Tabernacle are of immense value to our ability to effectively lead others to Jesus Christ.

When mankind committed the original sin against the commandments of God and was expelled from the Garden of Eden, even though God sent them forth from the garden, he never abandoned man. In God's grace and mercy, he used the tabernacle to demonstrate a system of redemption and to teach all humanity how even a sinful man could approach God and qualify for redemption. God had not altered His intended assignment man to have dominion over the works of His hands. Too often, today's believers base their outreach-offer of salvation in Jesus Christ on the benefits, advantages or plans of the sinner. That approach is based in selfishness, which violates a basic principle of God's kingdom. God redeemed man from sin based on his plan and purpose for mankind. He redeemed man to restore him to a position from which man could carry out God's original intent for him, and have dominion over the works of God's hands according to God plan in the first place. Understanding God's passion for his plan and purpose, demonstrated through his actions in this old tabernacle, will better equip modern day believer's to approach sinners with the idea of how the sinner's salvation will embrace the plan of God, and how the sinner will benefit when God's purpose and plans are working in the universe and in their lives.

The Old Testament Atonement

In this tabernacle, mankind for the first time is in need of redemption, the first phase was atonement. God gives a law in Leviticus 17:11, declaring that life of the flesh is in the blood and giving blood upon the altar to mankind to make atonement for sin.

This atonement process was initiated when the Old Testament man realized that his sin had caused separation between him and his God, and when he decided to be right with God again. When he arrived at this decision, he would secure his sacrificial offering and make his way through the camp of Israel, enter into the courtyard through the multicolored gate, leading his sacrificial animal behind him and present himself to the priests of God as a man needing forgiveness. He then laid his hands upon the animal's head confessed his sin this was to identify himself with his sacrifice because he realized that his sin could not be forgiven without the shedding of blood. The Torah, (first five books of the Bible) which had been taught to every Israeli from a child, had been very specific about that. *"For the life of the flesh is in the blood: and I have given it to you upon the altar to make atonement for your souls [spirit]: for it is the blood that maketh atonement for the soul" (Leviticus 17:11).* After laying his hands on the animal and receiving the prayers of the priest, the sinner, with knife in hand, would slash the throat of the animal. When the sinner slashed the animal's throat, it was the death of a sinless substitute dying for the guilty transgressor, the blood of the blameless being shed so that the guilt-ridden is spared.

And as the life-blood of the animal receded from its body, the sinful Israelite, sickened by the responsibility of personally slaying the animal, gained an unmistakable understanding of the fact that God had permitted the death of a substitute instead of his own death; he realized that sin is costly. Lastly, the Israelite had been taught and believed, that having been obedient to God's stated way of atonement his sin had in fact been atoned. Accepting God's Word, this man returned to his tent, fully confident that the separation between God and himself had been healed. Just how his sin could be removed by the exchange of the life of an animal for his own life was not fully understood; he knew only that he had done as God had directed and so he departed with a full sense of forgiveness.

Because the priests who ministered daily at the altar were mere men themselves, capable of sin, God's final words to the Old Testament people, including the priests of Israel, relating to this atonement ritual were these: *"So the priest shall make atonement for his sin that he has committed, and it shall be forgiven him" (Leviticus. 4:35).*

The words of God to Moses were very specific about how the Israelites were to approach God. They had never approached God while in the slave camps of Egypt; when God offered to reveal himself to the people at Mount Sinai, they were afraid and decided that no man except Moses could approach God. *"And all the people saw the thunderings, and the lightnings, and the noise of the trumpet, and the mountain smoking: and when the people saw it, they removed, and stood afar off. And they said unto Moses, Speak thou with us, and we will hear: but let not God speak with us, lest we die. And Moses said unto the people, Fear not: for God is come to prove you, and that his fear may be before your faces that ye sin not. And the people stood afar off, and Moses drew near unto the thick darkness where God was. And the Lord said unto Moses, Thus thou shalt say unto the children of Israel, Ye have seen that I have talked with you from heaven. Ye shall not make with me gods of silver, neither shall ye make unto you gods of gold" (Exodus 20:18–23).* Also read Exodus 19:7–25.

Nevertheless, God desired all Israel to become *a kingdom of priests* just as His instructions to his church today are to become a *kingdom of kings and priests*. God was never looking for Christians, and Jesus never preached to gain Christians. They were looking for citizens to occupy "the kingdom of God on earth". *"But, ye are a chosen generation, a royal priesthood, an holy nation, a peculiar people; that ye should show forth the praises of him who hath called you out of darkness into his marvelous light and come boldly to the throne of Grace" (1 Peter 2:9).* There in the Sinai wilderness, God used the Israeli nation to demonstrate an acceptable pattern for sinful man to approach God's presence. With this pattern of tabernacle worship, God began to reveal the arrangement of *substitutionary blood shed for the atonement of sin.* Thus, it was through this pattern of tabernacle worship that we first witnessed the approach to be used, for the redeeming, substitutionary, blood-sacrifice of Jesus Christ. Hallelujah!

We have used the much of our time during this study exploring and learning in detail how this tabernacle its ceremonies, rituals, and customs worked. Nevertheless without question, the most important knowledge given to us regarding mankind's salvation through Jesus Christ is this: **without the father's acceptance of the shed blood of the substitute animal sacrifices, mankind's sin-debt, had no process by which it could be paid.**

Sinful humanity, because of sin in the Garden of Eden was out of the will of Go, and could not then, and cannot now, save itself. But God in our weakness, arranged for redemption by the method of bringing the shed blood of a clean voluntary substitute to the altar. We also learned that perhaps the most perplexing truths for Old Testament mankind to grasp and fully comprehend was how the taking of the life of an innocent animal, on behalf of a sin-guilty person, makes the seeker of forgiveness righteous; or why this act would yield atonement or salvation by God. He had learned that: *the soul that sins, it shall surely die.*

Now, man learns that this Leviticus17:11 command of God allows him to offer a blood sacrifice at the altar and receive atonement. Even though he did not fully understand, he knew that God commanded it and his obedience was more profitable than disobedience: *"For the life of the flesh is in the blood: and I have given it to you upon the altar to make an atonement for your souls: for it is the blood that maketh an atonement for the soul."* Even though there will be times when we do not understand, it is still true: obedience is better than sacrifice.

Salvation in Jesus Christ

To begin to understand the salvation phenomenon, we must go back to the Garden of Eden. It was there in the book of Genesis that Adam, with all humankind locked inside his loins, violated God's commandment and caused a contamination that disqualified humanity from permanent uninterrupted relationship with God. Adam's sin aborted humanity's ability *to walk with God in the cool of the evening;* it destroyed mankind's fitness for use in God's original purpose for man.

In Genesis 1:26, the Lord God created the man in his image and likeness and gave him absolute dominion and authority with only one restriction: he was forbidden to eat from the tree of the knowledge of good and evil. However, everything that flew, swam, creeped or crawled was under Adam's dominion. Even that *serpent-being,* which slithered into the garden, was under Adam's authority. So Adam allowed this serpent-swindler to engage in the forbidden act of dialogue with his wife Eve. Even Jesus had no dialogue with the devil; he did, at appropriate times, command or rebuke him.

So, Adam, in his perfect state of control and dominion, allowed his wife to have dialogue with this creature who called God a liar (see Genesis 3:4). *"You will not surely die."* At no time during any of these various stages of disobedient activity did Adam make an effort to restrain either that serpent-being, or his wife. And Adam himself, with his eyes wide open, ate of the forbidden fruit and participated in this dreadful destructive activity. It is important to note that Adam was present at Eve's side when she was deceived by the serpent. Genesis 3:6: *"So when the woman saw that the tree was good for food, that it was pleasant to the eyes, and a tree desirable to make one wise, she took of its fruit and ate.* **She also gave to her husband with her,** *and he did eat."* Adam was not off some place fishing or picking grapes in a different part of the garden, when this awful transgression occurred. The apostle Paul makes it clear that Adam was not deceived: *"And Adam was not deceived, but the woman being deceived, fell into transgression"* (1 Timothy 2:14). Adam had received the Genesis 2:17 commandment: directly from God and knew that he was transgressing the command: *"But of the tree of the knowledge of good and evil, thou shalt not eat of it: for in the day that thou eatest thereof thou shalt surely die."* The consequences of Adam's actions were devastating for all mankind. By knowingly and willfully disobeying God, Adam literally aborted access to the spiritual power and dominion that God intended for mankind; and by his actions, he caused sin and death to reign on earth. *"For as by one man's [Adam's] disobedience many were made sinners, so by the obedience of one [Jesus] shall many be made righteous"* (Romans 5:19).

Through this atrocious act of disobedience, Satan legally became the ruler of this present visible world (cosmos). From that point forward, Satan, acting as [small "g"] *god of this world,* began to blind the minds of anyone who would listen, and mankind by the millions are still listening to the deceiver. *"But if our gospel be hid, it is hid to them that are lost: In whom the god of this his world hath blinded their minds of them which believe not, lest the light of the glorious gospel of Christ, who is the image of God, should shine unto them"* (2 Corinthians 4:3–4). The word *"world"* as used here is the Greek word *cosmos,* which literally means the world system.

This handover of power by Adam was the devil's basis to offer temptation to the Lord Jesus Christ on that high mountain where he offered to tempt the Lord. *"And the devil said unto him, all this power will I give thee, and the glory of them: for that is delivered unto me; and to whomsoever I will I give it. If thou therefore wilt worship me, all shall be thine. And Jesus answered and said unto him, Get thee behind me, Satan: for it is written, Thou shalt worship the Lord thy God, and him only shalt thou serve" (Luke 4:5–8.)*

It is in Genesis chapter three (3) where Adam openly violated the commandment of God; it is also here, that God gives a glimpse of the messianic advent. Here we find a subtle foretelling of the coming one. *"And I will put enmity [animosity] between you [Satan] and the woman and between your seed (demonic spirits and unrepentant mankind) and her seed [Messiah and spiritual mankind]; he shall bruise your head, and you shall bruise his heel" (Genesis 3:15).* The question of who is the devil's seed continues to be controversial. There is much debate among scholars about it, however, Jesus speaking to sinful men in the book of John, speaking to His opposers said this: *"Ye are of your father the devil and the lusts of your father ye will do. He was a murderer from the beginning, and abode not in the truth, because there is no truth in him. When he speaketh a lie, he speaketh of his own: for he is a liar and the father of it" (John 8:44).* It seems clear that sinners are the seed of the devil.

From this early *thread of messianic redemption* given in Genesis three, the promise of the coming messiah begins to unfold, and the unfolding continued until the method for delivery of the promise began to take physical form in specific and identifiable instructions, actions, rituals, and ceremonies in the tabernacle. Here, for the first time in the study of this old tabernacle record, we see God's initial requirements for redemption of sinful man. In order to return to God, the sinner needed a repentant heart, and a clean and acceptable blood-sacrifice. He had learned that without the shedding of blood there was no forgiveness for sin. However, now it is clear that the blood of a substitute rather than his own blood is acceptable to God. These early redemptive steps revealed in this old tabernacle gave to all mankind a better understanding of the path to be taken later by the savior of the world. Here, the pattern that God would use to bring the coming messiah into the earth was more fully demonstrated; and throughout the life and history of the nation of Israel they began to look for the coming king. The daily practices of the Israelite's in this earthly tabernacle made by the hands of man gave great insight as to the process that would allow a disobedient human race to return to God. These animal sacrifices made with the blood of bulls and goats the ashes of a heifer and the like, pointed the way for the coming messiah; however sin is a breach of the moral law, but these sacrifices belong to, the ceremonial law so these sacrifices provided only temporary ceremonial cleansing they were powerless to cleanse the conscience of mankind: *"For the law having a shadow of good things to come, and not the very image of the things, can never with those sacrifices which they offered year by year continually make the comers thereunto perfect. For then would they not have ceased to be offered? because that the worshippers once purged should have had no more conscience of sins. But in those sacrifices there is a remembrance again made of sins every year. For it is not possible that the blood of bulls and of goats should take away sins."* (Hebrews 10:1-4)

The process of eternal redemption necessary to cleanse not only the flesh, but also the conscience of sinful man, would be perfected by a much later act on a hill called Golgotha, on an old rugged cross. Redemption could only be fully accomplished by the shedding of the blood of the true Lamb of God, Jesus Christ. *"For if the blood of bulls and of goats, and the ashes of an heifer sprinkling the unclean, sanctifieth to the purifying of the flesh: How much more shall the blood of Christ, who through the eternal Spirit offered himself without spot to God, purge your conscience from dead works to serve the living God? And for this cause he is the mediator of the new testament, that by means of death, for the redemption of the transgressions that were under the first testament, they which are called might receive the promise of eternal inheritance"* (Hebrews 9:13-15).

BENEFITS OF THE BLOOD OF JESUS CHRIST

The first benefit for current-day humanity is to understand that Jesus Christ, the long awaited messiah, is the fulfillment of the Old Testament Tabernacle system. He is the genuine high priest sent forth from a superior priestly order, a sinless high priest who is therefore able to bring a final and lasting resolution for humanity's sin problem: *"For it is evident that our Lord sprang out of Judah; of which tribe Moses spake nothing concerning priesthood. And it is yet far more evident: for that after the similitude of Melchisedec there ariseth another priest, Who is made, not after the law of a carnal commandment, but after the power of an endless life. For he testifieth, Thou art a priest for ever after the order of Melchisedec. For there is verily a disannulling of the commandment going before for the weakness and unprofitableness thereof. For the law made nothing perfect, but the bringing in of a better hope did; by the which we draw nigh unto God. And inasmuch as not without an oath he was made priest: (For those priests were made without an oath; but this with an oath by him that said unto him, The Lord sware and will not repent, Thou art a priest for ever after the order of Melchisedec :(Hebrews 7:14-21)*

Unlike the Aaronic priests who, being mere men, committed sin and needed to atone for their personal transgressions, Jesus Christ had no sin problem of his own. *"But Christ being come an high priest of good things to come, by a greater and more perfect tabernacle, not made with hands, that is to say, not of this [earthly] building; Neither by the blood of goats and calves, but by his own blood he entered once into the holy place, having obtained eternal redemption for us all. For if the blood of bulls and of goats, and the ashes of a heifer sprinkling the unclean, sanctifieth to the purifying of the flesh: how much more shall the blood of Christ, who through the eternal spirit offered himself without spot to God, purge your conscience from dead works to serve the true and living God? And for this cause he is the mediator of the New Testament that by means of death, for the redemption of the transgressions that were under the first testament, they which are called might receive the promise of eternal inheritance"* (Hebrews 9:11–15).

Jesus went into the true tabernacle, into the throne room of heaven, the presence of the true and living God, and offered his own blood after voluntarily giving His life at Calvary and saying: *"No man taketh it [Jesus' life] from me, but I lay it down of myself. I have power to lay it down, and I have power to take it again. This commandment have I received of my father"* (John 10:18).

Christ became the perfect example of the innocent dying for the guilty, giving his own perfect and sinless life to pay the sin-debt for guilty mankind. Whereby he accomplished the permanent solution of salvation, for anyone who believes and embraces his work on the cross; he died once for all time for all mankind. The Old Testament sacrifices could only accomplish ritualistic, ceremonial cleansing, and the atonement they brought was temporary; but the sacrifice made by Jesus Christ obliterates sin, removes guilt, and cleanses the conscious of man from sin, which allows man to freely worship God and by his spirit enter his personal presence. This is why Jesus, just before he died on the cross, cried with a loud voice, *"It is finished"* (Matt.27:50; John 19:30). He meant by this saying that all the Old Testament sacrifices are finished; the whole bloody tabernacle system of killing goats, and bulls, and heifers is finished; the secret confessions of man to a human priest is finished; the inability of the priests of God to live sinless lives is finished; all of what was symbolized by this old system is now accomplished. In the moment when Jesus gave up the ghost (died), the veil of separation that hung between God and mankind was torn from top to bottom: *"Jesus, when he had cried again with a loud voice, yielded up the ghost. And, behold, the veil of the temple was rent in twain from the top to the bottom; and the earth did quake, and the rocks rent" (Matthew 27:50–51).*

The veil of separation between humanity and God had stood since Adam [man] sinned in the garden, and continued to stand until Jesus died because the blood of bulls and goats was powerless to gain humanity's access to the Holy of Holies. Animal blood was powerless to cleanse man's consciousness and provide permanent salvation. But now the separation has been bridged and direct access into God's presence is open to all mankind: *"Seeing then that we have a great high priest that is passed into the heavens, Jesus the son of God; let us hold fast our profession, for we have not an high priest which cannot be touched with the feeling of our infirmities; but was in all points tempted as we are, yet without sin. Let us therefore come boldly unto the throne of grace that we may obtain mercy, and find grace to help in time of need" (Hebrews 4:14-16).* The sins of mankind are obliterated, his conscious is cleansed, and his life can now be aligned to God's purpose. ***"For if the blood of bulls and of goats, and the ashes of a heifer sprinkling the unclean, sanctifieth to the purifying of the flesh: how much more shall the blood of Christ, who through the eternal spirit offered himself without spot to God, purge your conscience from dead works to serve the living God?" (Hebrews 9:13–14).***

To personally accept the benefits of Jesus' shed blood at Calvary, first one must hear and understand His gospel, that is to say, the good news of what Jesus accomplished that culminated with His resurrection following Calvary. Then one must truly believe that they are personally included among the recipients of the benefits of his redemptive work, and embrace the fact that father God accepted the blood of Jesus as payment for your sin-debt. Further, one must repent for past sins, and make the commitment to daily seek God's direction for your life from this point forward. Many ask how to seek his directions. God's direction is discovered by studying his Word; He gives instructions for life in the scriptures. Finally, ask God to accept you into his family and grant you salvation in Jesus Christ. You will also want to find a scripture-teaching church.

Sin separates us from God and renders us worthy of the same full force of his judgment as was applied to Jesus, when he became sin for the whole world. As you grow in understanding by daily study of the Word of God, you will receive from the spirit a desire to worship God. The word will also teach you that sin separates you from God. "*Behold, the Lord's hand is not shortened, that it cannot save; neither his ear heavy that it cannot hear: but your iniquities [sins] have separated between you and your God, and your sins have hid his face from you, that he will not hear. For your hands are defiled with blood, and your fingers with iniquity; your lips have spoken lies, your tongue hath muttered perverseness. None calleth for justice, nor any pleadeth for truth: they trust in vanity, and speak lies; they conceive mischief, and bring forth iniquity. They hatch cockatrice' eggs, and weave the spider's web: he that eateth of their eggs dieth, and that which is crushed breaketh out into a viper*" (Isaiah 59:1–5).

SPIRITUAL ESSENCE OF THE EARTHLY TABERNACLE

This old tabernacle of Moses is not to be seen as a rich source for symbolic imagination; we must view it as scripture-based revelation teaching us, among other things, how God dealt with sinful humankind following the fall (original sin). Rather than guessing about symbolic connections between tabernacle details and the Messiah's work, we must look to the scriptures to understand how the tabernacle relates to Jesus Christ. With an astute comprehension of the tabernacle we are equipped to understand the New Testament and how Jesus Christ, our Messiah, fulfilled the requirements of God for redemption revealed to mankind through the Tabernacle experience.

We learned earlier that in Old Testament days, the tabernacle here on earth was the dwelling place of God. However, with the occurrence of the death, burial, and resurrection work of Jesus Christ, God no longer dwells in an earthly building. He now dwells in the believer by his spirit: *"And I will pray the father, and he shall give you another comforter, that he may abide with you forever; even the spirit of truth; whom the world cannot receive, because it seeth [perceives] him not, neither knoweth [has full faith in his work] him: but ye know him; for he dwelleth with you, and shall be in you."* (John 14:16)

Also see John 16:7: *"Nevertheless, I tell you the truth; it is expedient for you that I go away: for if I go not away, the Comforter will not come unto you; but if I depart, I will send him unto you."*

So, whereas the old Tabernacle was God's first dwelling place on earth, that old symbolism was fulfilled (replaced) through the death burial and resurrection work of Christ the Messiah, whereby now true believers are the temple of God. *"Know ye not that ye are the temple of God, and that the spirit of God dwelleth in you?" (1Corinthians 3:16).*

The foreshadowing types of the Old Testament sacrifices made at the brazen altar were fulfilled at Messiah's death. Jesus Christ became the authentic sacrifice; required to produce a better covenant providing for the cleansing and purification of mankind's conscious. The power of his blood exceeded what was need for purification of the old sanctuary; His blood was powerful enough to renew man's mind, deliver purification of the conscious of humanity, and create a pathway for man directly into God's presence. *"Now when these things were thus ordained, the priests went always into the first tabernacle, accomplishing the service of God. But into the second went the high priest alone once every year, not without blood, which he offered for himself, and for the errors of the people: The Holy Ghost this signifying, that the way into the holiest of all was not yet made manifest, while as the first tabernacle was yet standing: Which was a figure for the time then present, in which were offered both gifts and sacrifices, that could not make him that did the service perfect, as pertaining to the conscience; Which stood only in meats and drinks, and divers washings, and carnal ordinances, imposed on them until the time of reformation. But Christ being come an high priest of good things to come, by a greater and more perfect tabernacle, not made with hands, that is to say, not of this building; Neither by the blood of goats and calves, but by his own blood he entered in once into the holy place, having obtained eternal redemption for us" (Hebrews. 9:6–12).*

The old ***"bread of the presence (shewbread)"*** that sat continually before the presence of God, thus being immersed in his essence, is replaced by Jesus Christ as he sits at the right hand of the father day and night making intercessions for the believers. The sacrificial blood of Jesus made it possible for all who have faith in his redemptive work at Calvary's cross, to live continually day and night in his presence by his spirit.

The Menorah was a symbol of light, illuminating God's glory in the Holy Place; it is replaced because Messiah; is the light of the world and is the father's glory to all who will follow him. *"We beheld his glory, the glory of the father" (John 1:14).* Also, see Hebrews: *"Who being the brightness of his glory, and the express image of his person, and upholding all things by the word of his power, when he had by himself purged our sins, sat down on the right hand of the Majesty on high" (Hebrews 1:3).*

The Incense: The cloud of smoke created by the burning incense protected the high priest from direct face-to-face contact with God, while he ministered in the presence of his holiness; such face-to-face contact with God was forbidden to flesh and would bring death. See Exodus: *"And he said, Thou canst not see my face: for there shall no man see me, and live" (Exodus 33:20).* So Jesus by the spirit has become our protection as we come boldly into his presence to the throne of God's grace. When the veil was rent (torn) by his death, he made the way for us to draw near to God. See Mark: *"And the veil of the temple was rent in twain from the top to the bottom. And when the centurion, which stood over against him saw, that he so cried out, and gave up the ghost, he said, Truly this man was the Son of God" (Mark 15:38–39).* Also see Hebrews: *"Seeing then that we have a great high priest, that is passed into the heavens, Jesus the Son of God, let us hold fast our profession. For we have not an high priest which cannot be touched with the feeling of our infirmities; but was in all points tempted like as we are, yet without sin. Let us therefore come boldly unto the throne of grace that we may obtain mercy, and find grace to help in time of need" (Hebrews 4:14–16).*

The Ark of the Covenant where the tablets containing the Ten Commandments, called the Law of Moses, and other memorable items were stored, has been replaced. Jesus gave a new commandment after the shedding his blood at Calvary's cross. *"A new commandment I give unto you, That ye love one another; as I have loved you, that ye also love one another. By this shall all men know that ye are my disciples, if ye have love one to another" (1 Peter 2:5, 9).* See also Hebrews: *"By a new and living way, which he hath consecrated for us, through the veil, that is to say, his flesh; And having an high priest over the house of God; Let us draw near with a true heart in full assurance of faith, having our hearts sprinkled from an evil conscience, and our bodies washed with pure water. Let us hold fast the profession of our faith without wavering; (for he is faithful that promised" (Hebrews 10:20-23).* Also see 1 Corinthians: *"After the same manner also he took the cup, when he had supped, saying, this cup is the new testament in my blood: this do ye, as often as ye drink it, in remembrance of me" (1 Corinthians 11:25).*

The Manna, also stored inside the *Ark of the Covenant* as a memorial of the bread, which God gave to feed the nation of Israel, the people of God, in the Sinai wilderness, is replaced by Jesus who is the bread of life. See John 6: *"And Jesus said unto them, I am the bread of life: he that cometh to me shall never hunger; and he that believeth on me shall never thirst" (John 6:35).*

Aaron's rod that budded was also stored in the Ark as a remembrance of when God settled the dispute regarding what tribe would be leader in the camp of the Tabernacle (read Numbers chapter 17). Aaron's rod also points to Jesus. *"And the Lord said unto Moses, 'Bring Aaron's rod again before the testimony, to be kept for a token against the rebels; and thou shalt quite, take away their murmurings from me, that they die not.' And Moses did so: as the Lord commanded him, so did he" (Numbers 17:10-11)* However, now the King of kings and Lord of lords has come, and there are no further disputes about the leader of God's people. *"But now hath he obtained a more excellent ministry, by how much also he is the mediator of a better covenant, which was established upon better promises." (Hebrews*

8:6). Jesus is God's manifested presence; He has sent the Holy Spirit, the comforter, to help and empower believers to live in the *kingdom of God on earth.* So, that old Ark of the Covenant, which found its place inside the holy of holies in the tabernacle on earth, is no longer a standard for God's people. *"And it shall come to pass, when ye be multiplied and increased in the land, in those days, saith the Lord, they shall say no more, the ark of the covenant of the Lord: neither shall it come to mind: neither shall they remember it; neither shall they visit it; neither shall that be done any more" (Jeremiah 3:16).*

The crown of gold around the top of the ark speaks of Jesus Christ as King of kings and Lord of lords. Jesus overcame the onslaught of opposition that was set against him during his entire time on earth by the religious leaders and the wealthy aristocracy, by Rome itself, and even by the power of Satan. Nevertheless, He overcame the cross, death, and the grave, and rose triumphantly with all power and glory and honor. He is undeniably king, prophet, and priest; King of Kings and Lord of Lords forever.

The prophet Isaiah wrote about Jesus, seated on the throne in heaven with the angels around him crying, "Holy, holy, holy." See Isaiah 6: *"And one cried unto another, and said, holy, holy, holy, is the Lord of hosts: the whole earth is full of his glory" (Isaiah 6:3).*

The unbroken stone tablets of the Ten Commandments remind us of Jesus who perfectly kept the law and never broke God's commandments. The Bible says that *"he committed no sin, nor was deceit found in his mouth" (1 Peter 2:22).* Jesus experienced the full intensity of temptation yet he never sinned. His very presence personified and portrayed obedience and perfection to the holiness of God.

It all points to Jesus. Even the golden poles that never left the sides of the ark speak of the ever-living and ever-present savior who is with us in all our journeying through life. He will never leave us or forsake us.

Finally, we are reminded that at the core of the tabernacle was the treasured Ark of the Covenant, with its mercy seat, atop which God himself sat; this ark and mercy seat was located at the precise center of the entire tabernacle camp and all its activities. A close examination of scripture regarding the history of the ark reveals striking resemblances between this Old Testament ark and the ministry of Jesus Christ.

This sacred ark went before the people of God; Jesus went before the people of God: *"And when he putteth forth his own sheep he goeth before them, and the sheep follow him: for they know his voice" (John 10:4)*. The following scriptures are for your meditation:

"For unto us a child is born, unto us a son is given; and the government shall be upon his shoulder. And his name shall be called wonderful counselor, mighty God, everlasting father, prince of peace" (Isaiah 9:6).

"Do not think that I came to destroy the law or the prophets. I did not come to destroy but to fulfill" (Matthew 5:17).

"For even hereunto were ye called: because Christ also suffered for us, leaving us an example, that ye should follow his steps: Who did no sin, neither was guile found in his mouth" (1 Peter 2:21–22).

"But when the fullness of the time was come, God sent forth his son, made of a woman, made under the law, to redeem them that were under the law, that we might receive the adoption of sons" (Galatians 4:4–5).

"Jesus said unto her, I am the resurrection, and the life: he that believeth in me, though he were dead, yet shall he live: And whosoever liveth and believeth in me shall never die. Believest thou this?" (John 11:25–26).

"And the Word became flesh and dwelt among us, and we beheld his glory, the glory as of the only begotten of the father, full of grace and truth" (John 1:14).

The Ark of the Covenant located in the old tabernacle of Moses here on earth was symbolic of the real ark, God's throne in heaven.

Faith and the Blood of Jesus

Current-day believers are taught to embrace the natural earthy logical intellectual realm of life and to be leery of the spiritual realm; however, mankind's only avenue for access to God comes through our spiritual acceptance of the voluntary blood sacrifice of Jesus Christ on our behalf. Only by spiritual faith that is a spiritual operation in our lives, are we able to fully comprehend that: *"God is a Spirit: and they that worship him must worship him in spirit and in truth" (John 4:24)*. Only by spiritual faith are we able to embrace Jesus Christ as our redeemer. Only by faith in the truth of God's word are we immerse or baptized into the enabling power of the Holy Spirit.

It is by faith that we know that Christ was humanity's substitute-on-the-cross, dying in our stead; and it is by faith that we understand that Jesus now lives in and through the believer, by the spirit of God, to accomplish God's will on earth. The apostle Paul expresses the required level of faith in Galatians, the true believer must comprehend and be able to say: *"I am crucified with Christ: nevertheless I live; yet not I, but Christ liveth in me: and the life which I now live in the flesh I live by the faith of the son of God, who loved me, and gave himself for me" (Galatians 2:20)*. The scripture, here in Galatians 2:20, is a reference to the sacrificial substitution by Jesus; while Christendom often speaks about sacrificial substitution, the less than clear teaching on this principle has left it mysterious and confusing for many believers. In mankind's folly we embrace the popular path and live as debtors to the natural flesh, rather than choosing to walk after the spirit, live by faith and enjoy the peace that Jesus' death provided. Remember Romans chapter 8, *"There is therefore now no condemnation to them which are in Christ Jesus, who walk not after the flesh, but after the Spirit."* And Jesus said, *"Peace I leave with you, my peace I give unto you: not as the world giveth, give I unto you. Let not your heart be troubled, neither let it be afraid" (John 14:7).*

Look at this passage in Colossians: *"For ye are dead, and your life is hid with Christ in God. When Christ, who is our life, shall appear, then shall ye also appear with him in glory, mortify therefore your members which are upon the earth; fornication, uncleanness, inordinate affections, evil concupiscence, and covetousness, which is idolatry: for which things' sake the wrath of God cometh on the children of disobedience: In the which ye also walked some time, when ye lived in them. But now ye also put off all these; anger, wrath, malice, blasphemy, filthy communication out of your mouth. Lie not one to another, seeing that ye have put off the old man with his deeds; and have put on the new man, which is renewed in knowledge after the image of him that created him: Where there is neither Greek nor Jew, circumcision nor uncircumcision, barbarian, scythian, bond nor free: but Christ is all, and in all. Put on therefore, as the elect of God, holy and beloved, bowels of mercies, kindness, humbleness of mind, meekness, longsuffering; forbearing one another, and forgiving one another, if any man have a quarrel against any: even as Christ forgave you, so also do ye. And above all these things put on charity (love), which is the bond of perfectness. And let the peace of God rule in your hearts, to the which also ye are called in one body; and be ye thankful. Let the word of Christ dwell in you richly in all wisdom; teaching and admonishing one another in psalms and hymns and spiritual songs, singing with grace in your hearts to the Lord. And whatsoever ye do in word or deed, do all in the name of the Lord Jesus, giving thanks to God and the father by him" (Colossians 3:3–17).*

A true believer is a changed person, ready by faith to submit their fleshly desires to the master; these desires lead to so much unnecessary drama, heartache, and pain that are released when we realize and accept the reality of Jesus Christ as our substitute, and accept the fact that the believer's life is hidden with Christ in God. This principle of Christ as the believer's substitute is imbedded throughout the fabric of the New Testament. The Lord himself mentions this substitutionary life: *"I will not leave you comfortless: I will come to you. Yet a little while, and the world seeth me no more; but ye see me: because I live, ye shall live also. At that day ye shall know that I am in my father, and ye in me, and I in you" (John 14:18–20).*

Notice that in verse 18 he says, *"I will not leave you comfortless: **I will come to you**.* "Christ uses the same word to refer to himself as used in John 14:16–17 to mean the Holy Spirit. Notice Jesus is not saying here the spirit will come, he says ***"I will come,"*** identifying himself as being one with the Holy Spirit. In verse 19, he says, *"Because I live, ye shall live also."* He doesn't say you will live because you live in a certain neighborhood, or because you have a sizable bank account, or have a certain education. He doesn't identify you according to anything apart from himself. But by virtue of the fact that, as the spirit of God now lives and works through your life, and because your condition is, as he is, you shall live also. See 1 John 4:17: *"Herein is our love made perfect, that we may have boldness in the day of judgment: because as he is, so are we in this his world."*

This is life, and faith in Christ, based on a greater understanding of the substitution process. The two most important events connected to substitutionary life are (1) when Jesus Christ himself shed his blood on the cross paying the sin-debt for all mankind; and (2) when he performs his will, in and through believers on earth. It is Christ as the life-giving spirit, being all and doing all through the believer. If this to be a reality in an individual's life, that person must understand and accept by faith, the basic principle that Jesus gave his life, that those who believe, might have life abundantly and that Christ by the Spirit of the Father, might accomplish their work here on earth through the believer. Again, hear the voice of God through the apostle Paul: *"I am crucified with Christ: nevertheless I live; yet not I, but Christ liveth in me: and the life which I now live in the flesh I live by the faith of the Son of God, who loved me, and gave himself for me"* (Galatians 2:20).

Where are the Current-Day Priests?

When we ask the question, *where are the current-day priests?* I am reminded of the historical record of Abraham's son Isaac as he spoke to his father in Genesis 22:7 saying: *"Behold the fire and the wood: but where is the lamb for a burnt offering?"* Isaac was saying, *I see the wood for the fire but where is the sacrificial lamb to be used for the burnt offering?*

As we have studied the Old Testament Tabernacle, we have learned it was a pre-shadowing of things to come, an earthy structure made of wood covered with gold, brass, curtains dyed with selected colors and skins of different animals.

We clearly understood that there were substitute-animal sacrifices i.e. bulls, goats, heifers etc. We were also aware of the repenting sinners, and a forgiving God; however, there were also priests who ministered before God. So, now that the old tabernacle is abolished, we should find an authentic replacement for those Old Testament types and shadows. As we read the New Testament, by faith, we find the same loving God now seated on his actual throne; by faith we see the replacement for the sacrifices, the Lamb of God, Jesus Christ, the spiritual reality. We can identify the repenting sinners in current-day unregenerate mankind. What seems to be missing is a current-day authentic replacement for the old tabernacle priesthood of God. Throughout the study of the

Tabernacle of Moses, we watched the priests minister between God and the people. Also during this study, we found time and time again that this Old Testament tabernacle and all that was connected with it were just a shadow of the *reality to come later*. We also learned that the bulls, goats, pigeons, doves, etc. were types of *sacrificial innocents*, dying for the guilty. These animal sacrifices were replaced when Jesus Christ, the true and effective sacrificial lamb, shed his own blood and made redemption available for all mankind for all time. We can see that the old tabernacle Israelite who recognized that sin in his life separated him from his God and made his way through the tabernacle gate to the sacrificial altar of burnt offerings, is replaced by current-day unrepented mankind coming spiritually and by faith to the sacrificial altar of the cross of Christ, for salvation. But where are the current-day replacements for the old tabernacle *priesthood of God?*

There are certain groups where men dress in robes and are called priests. But upon examination, we find that these priests are a continuation of the old Aaronic priesthood; these priests are still mere men capable of sin and, on regular basis, need forgiveness for themselves; these characteristics render them ineffective to stand in the gap between God and mankind. So where do we find priests, after the higher order of Jesus Christ or Melchisedec, both called priest after the order of the most high God: *"So also Christ glorified not himself to be made an high priest; but he that said unto him, Thou art my Son, today have I begotten thee. As he saith also in another place, Thou art a priest forever after the order of Melchisedec. Who in the days of his flesh, when he had offered up prayers and supplications with strong crying and tears unto him that was able to save him from death, and was heard in that he feared"* (Hebrews 5:5-7). Where are the priests, who are qualified to bring about a connection, between God and humanity at any given time or place? Where are the replacements, the reality, for those tabernacle priests who ministered between God and the people?

A careful reading of the scriptures reveals that it was always the purpose and plan of God that those who are redeemed by the blood of Jesus, the believers, would become the current-day reality to reign on earth as replacements for the tabernacle priesthood. Father God throughout scripture, references the believers in Christ as spiritual replacements for the old tabernacle priest. See 1 Peter 2:5: *"Ye also, as lively stones, are built up a spiritual house, a holy priesthood, to offer up spiritual sacrifices, acceptable to God by Jesus Christ."* Also see 1 Peter 2:9: *"But ye are a chosen generation, a royal priesthood, a holy nation, a peculiar people; that ye should shew forth the praises of him who hath called you out of darkness into his marvelous light."* And Revelation 5: *"And they sung a new song, saying, Thou art worthy to take the book, and to open the seals thereof: for thou (Jesus) was slain, and hast redeemed us (believers) to God by thy blood out of every kindred, and tongue, and people, and nation; And hast made us unto our God kings and priests: and we shall reign on the earth"* (Revelation 5:9–10). Where were we led astray? How have we come to this place where somehow believers have relinquished their *office of the priesthood* in exchange for the title of Christian; God was never seeking Christians, he was always interested in building his kingdom on earth and populating it with *kingdom citizens,* all of whom would be priests to the all mighty God. Also, Jesus never preached or taught about Christians; He taught about the kingdom. Mankind got it twisted and believers like sheep that have gone astray, have moved into a position that is far beneath their privileges. This revelatory knowledge has been a hidden secret to most believers for their entire Christian life; for the most part, believers are unaware that they are the *"new reality priesthood"* that was hidden in Christ. Just as the priests of the old tabernacle had certain prescribed duties to assure that their ministry on behalf of humanity was acceptable to God, now believers, as a royal priesthood, a holy nation, a peculiar people, must accept the priestly responsibility on earth, for ministry on behalf of mankind that is acceptable to God. Let's look at the responsibility of the believers as the replacement reality priesthood on earth.

Duties of the Priesthood

As we observe the priesthood of the old tabernacle, we notice that intercessory and ministry responsibilities were exclusively the prerogative of the priests, God commanded it and the people believed that only the priest possessed the anointing and the degree of holiness fitting to approach the holy spaces of the sanctuary and/or the altars. The priests were responsible to bear, carry the ark of the covenant of the Lord, and to stand before the Lord and minister on behalf of the people. However, we know, that all changed when the veil was rent at the death of Jesus; and now all believers have access to the required degree of holiness, to come boldly unto the throne of grace for worship or intercession, that we may obtain mercy, and find grace to help in time of need. In the old tabernacle, God's presence resided atop the Ark of the Covenant on the mercy seat between the cherubim. This Ark of the Covenant with its mercy seat in the holy of holies is where the high priest ministered before God on behalf of the people. That natural, earthly Ark of the Covenant and its mercy seat, where God's presence dwelled for that present time, was a foreshadowing of God's current dwelling place on earth, which is in the spirit of the true believer. As current-day believer/priests we must accept the priestly responsibility, by faith we must carry the genuine spiritual *Ark of the Covenant* perpetually in our spirit (often interpreted heart), as we remain anointed by his spirit and capable of making or facilitating a connection with God on behalf of ourselves or the people of the earth.

As the natural human high priest entered into the holy of holies beyond the veil once a year and ministered on behalf of the nation of Israel, the current-day believer/priesthood must stand ready before the

Lord daily to minister and pronounce blessings upon a sick and dying world. The tabernacle priests also carried and established the physical tabernacle, the place where humans via the high priest could meet with God. Now believers as priests of the most high God are ordained to carry the meeting place of God in their heart, by his spirit. *"Only thou shalt not number the tribe of Levi [the priestly tribe], neither take the sum of them among the children of Israel: But thou shalt appoint the Levites over the tabernacle of testimony, and over all the vessels thereof, and over all things that belong to it: they shall bear the tabernacle, and all the vessels thereof; and they shall minister unto it, and shall encamp round about the tabernacle. And when the tabernacle setteth forward [move from one place to another] the Levites (priestly tribe) shall take it down: and when the tabernacle is to be pitched [set up or reestablished], the Levites shall set it up: and the stranger that cometh nigh shall be put to death"* (Numbers 1:49–53).

The present-day believer/priest must view and recognize that the events and circumstances of their daily lives are divinely arranged occurrences, assignments, ordained by God. And when God brings people, or circumstances, across their path, they must view that as an opportunity for God to inhabit and divinely intervene into that moment. In other words, believer/priests have now become the walking, breathing, meeting place of God on earth, a tabernacle, a spiritual dwelling place among God's people. Believers are the spiritual mediators through whom God and humanity can meet. As God's priests, wherever believers are becomes a spiritual Wi-Fi hot spot for God's presence; a place where mankind can plug into and connect with their maker. As believer/priests, you have accepted the duty to facilitate meetings between God and humanity. When you are in the grocery store, your presence presents an opportunity for the store manager, the stockperson, or another shopper to connect and experience a spiritual encounter with God. Real priests of God are able to discern the movement of God's spirit, and wherever God moves, they move; and wherever the cloud settles, they settle and set up camp for ministry, always prepared to minister before their God. Believers must understand that the laws of the Old Testament Tabernacle and its priesthood has been disannulled and replaced by the Priesthood of Jesus Christ; and just as the sons of Aaron were made earthy priests, the sons of God are now made spiritual priests after the order of Jesus Christ. Read Hebrews 5:1-6: *"For every high priest taken from among men is ordained for men in things pertaining to God, that he may offer both gifts and sacrifices for sins: Who can have compassion on the ignorant, and on them that are out of the way; for that he himself also is compassed with infirmity. And by reason hereof he ought, as for the people, so also for himself, to offer for sins. And no man taketh this honour unto himself, but he that is called of God, as was Aaron. So also Christ glorified not himself to be made an high priest; but he that said unto him, Thou art my Son, today have I begotten thee. As he saith also in another place, Thou art a priest for ever after the order of Melchisedec".* Then read Hebrews 7: 14-21: *"For it is evident that our Lord sprang out of Judah; of which tribe Moses spake nothing concerning priesthood. And it is yet far more evident: for that after the similitude of Melchisedec there ariseth another priest, who is made, not after the law of a carnal commandment, but after the power of an endless life. For he testifieth, Thou art a priest for ever after the order of Melchisedec. For there is verily a disannulling of the commandment going before for the weakness and unprofitableness thereof. For the law made nothing perfect, but the bringing in of a better hope did; by the which we draw nigh unto God. And inasmuch as not without an oath he was made priest: For those priests were made without an oath; but this with an oath by him that said unto him, The Lord sware and will not repent, Thou art a priest for ever after the order of Melchisedec."* My prayer and encouragement for all believers is that they will understand and embrace the mantle of the priesthood after the order of Jesus Christ; that they search out and embrace their true identity and responsibility as a believer/priest of the most high God; that they recognize they are carriers of the *Ark of the Covenant,* that upon the mercy seat of your spirit, sits the very presence of God and you must stand ready to speak to God on behalf of the people, and to speak to the people on behalf of God at all times.

The time has come for a new awakening in the kingdom of God. I believe that God is saying, *Believers must mature and accept the responsibility to perpetually walk in the blessings, authority, and power of God, and to fully understand that true believers are ordained by God to carry the mantle of his blessings, authority, and power.* That is the message of 2 Corinthians 5: *"Now then we are ambassadors for Christ, as though God did beseech you by us: we pray you in Christ's stead, be ye reconciled to God" (2 Corinthians 5:20).* God sees every believer made in his own image and likeness, as a priest after the order of Jesus Christ with priestly responsibilities in the earth. True believers are but heavenly pilgrims passing through this lost world; they are diplomats, with full diplomatic immunity from the laws of earth, dispatched here by God, to save this place. *And no one and no thing, except God or we ourselves, can have dominion over us, or can restrict or limit us to the standards of this present day earthly kingdom.* Any effort to restrict the authority of a believer/priest of the most high God to the laws of this present visible earthly kingdom, is a violation of divine and universal sovereignty. Think about it. Any natural earthly governmental ambassador-diplomat represents the power and authority of his home country, and wherever such an ambassador travels, the power and authority of the home country government goes with him or her; wherever he or she set their foot, temporarily becomes the territory of his or her home country. Likewise, wherever true believers set their foot, temporarily becomes the territory of the invisible kingdom of God; and while you are there, the authority and power of the kingdom of God, are in full effective operation; the laws of earth are suspended, for that time, in that place.

Believer/priests, as kingdom ambassadors, are to call those things that be not, as though they were: *"As it is written, I have made thee a father of many nations, before him whom he believed, even God, who quickeneth the dead, and calleth those things which be not as though they were"* *(Romans 4:17).* Believers are anointed by faith in the authority of God to lay hands on the sick or hurting and expect them to recover. When an authentic believer/priest of God walks into a sick room, the laws of sickness, pain, and death no longer have authority in that place. *"For the law of the Spirit of life in Christ Jesus hath made me free from the law of sin and death"(Romans 8:2).*

When a priest of the most high God lay hands on the sick, the laws of the kingdom of God make null and void the powers of the laws of the kingdom of darkness. ***A priest, after the order of Jesus Christ carrying the anointing, presence, authority, and power of God,*** has entered the room. And in this room, the laws of the kingdom of God prevail. *"They shall take up serpents [problems not snakes]; and if they drink any deadly thing, it shall not hurt them; they shall lay hands on the sick, and they shall recover"* *(Mark 16:18).* The laws of sickness must yield to the laws of health and wellness; pain must make way for comfort and healing; death departs to make way for abundant life. When an ambassador/priest enters the room and enforces his/her reign they draw upon the resources of his/her home country, the kingdom of heaven and change is manifested.

My greatest desire in producing this tabernacle work is that the reader will discover, or rediscover, some truth here that will enlarge or expand their understanding of God's Word, and of his purpose for arranging your conception, birth, physical, mental, and spiritual growth so far. Further, it is my desire that because of your deeper understanding, you will be truly open to God's leading and direction; fully aware that the father may choose you for the deep, life-altering experience, of fully submitting your human spirit to the rule of the Holy Spirit; the precious third person of the godhead. I encourage you to embrace his direction for your life and live at peace here and in the life to come.

May the blessings of God flow richly to your life, family, and work in his kingdom.

Epilogue

The Tabernacle of Moses: the Prototype for Salvation in Jesus Christ" shares and explains ancient mysteries hidden by God in his Word, secrets revealed only to those who diligently seek his revelation. Proverbs 25:2 tells us: *"It is the glory of God to conceal a thing: but the honour of kings (believers as kings and priests) is to search out a matter"*. It is one thing to read about godly revelation; it is another thing to personally receive and comprehend godly revelation. And still quite another thing to walk in the discipline needed to live in obedience to godly revelation; and it is something else altogether to help others comprehend his revelation.

Insight into God's ways, his will, and his Word may come in a variety of ways: by study of his word, hearing his word, inspiration by the holy spirit, or sometimes simply by observing God's amazing creation. No matter how the godly insight arrives, when it comes, your mind is stretched and old ways are challenged by new insight into the *"incredibleness"* that is God. New godly revelation demands new actions that propels the receiver to a new place in God, beyond mere intellectual existence. Now, your mind, will, appetites, emotions, and spirit must become aligned and engaged in the determination to conform your life to your new awareness, moving you from the arena of natural academia and logic into the realm of an authentic spiritual existence: to a new place where character is forged, outlook is focused, and people around you are positively impacted. You are now required to become one of a rare few human beings on earth, who finally get beyond themselves to a place where pretense has now met its death; a place where you become acquainted with a new humbleness that allows you to honestly touch the hem of his garment and discover genuine joy and authentic fulfillment unlike anything you have experienced before. It is my belief that reading *The Tabernacle of Moses: the Prototype for Salvation in Jesus Christ has* imparted to your life deep insightful knowledge of how the Old and New Testament scriptures work and has equipped you to comprehend what the scriptures say and, more importantly, what they really mean. I have endeavored to provide documentation to y support your faith stance and show how your life will benefit from true godly revelation.

The joy, peace, and prosperity you experience from a true understanding of the Word of God will be amazingly multiplied within your circle of family, friends, and the community of faith. Your new life will please the heart of God. You have dared to explore beyond yourself to comprehend the historical truths of this Old Testament structure and its essentialness to the salvation of current-day believers. More importantly, you now have a grasp of authentic biblical principles and their historical background this knowledge unwraps your ability to study and comprehend God's Word for as long as you shall live. I urge you never again to settle for a mere understanding of what the Word said, but strive until you comprehend what is meant by what it said. Thank you and God bless you.

Dr. Henry Horton

Dr. Horton can be reached for conference speaking, workshops, seminars, or provisionally filling the pulpit.

(1) Tabernacle teachings
(2) Pastoral training
(3) Church Board/staff training
(4) Marriage advisory seminars
(5) Church development workshops, etc.

henryhorton025@gmail.com